D1431339

THE POWER OF THE HOLY SPIRIT

VOL. II

DON DeWELT
Professor at Ozark Bible College
Joplin, Missouri

College Press, Joplin, Missouri

PREFACE

Please Read This

I am so indebted to other writers in this area of study I hardly know which is mine, and which is theirs. In a very real sense I feel nothing is mine. ("Nought have I gotten but what I received.") Many points of emphasis, many comparative scripture references I have found in the writings of another. I claim no originality for this material. If you feel you have read some of this before, it is probably because you have. I have given credit wherever I knew it was due. When I have forgotten or overlooked a source, I beg patience. Write to me about any reference and I shall be more than glad to grant honor where honor is due.

Many readers have not access to the books here mentioned or the time to read them. I have both. Much of this material is a result of careful research. It is sent forth with but one purpose— *to help us all to be filled with joy and the Holy Spirit.* (Acts 13:52)

Don DeWelt

April, 1966

DEDICATION

To Jean — an
answer to prayer

INTRODUCTION

We propose a thorough study of the subject of the Holy Spirit, i.e. a consideration of every reference in the Bible on the subject. Whereas this will be a thorough study it shall also be very practical and personal. We shall study the subject in thirteen lessons as follows:

1. Who is the Holy Spirit?

2. Do all Christians possess the Holy Spirit?

3. How can the Holy Spirit help me?

4. Should I be baptized in the Holy Spirit?

5. Should I speak in tongues?

6. How can I be filled with the Holy Spirit?

7. How can I have the fruit of the Spirit?

8. Can the Holy Spirit help me to overcome sin?

9. How did the Holy Spirit help Christ? Is this an example for me?

10. How did the Holy Spirit inspire the writers of the Bible?

11. How can I be led of the Holy Spirit?

12. What about the Holy Spirit in the Old Testament?

13. What is the blasphemy of the Holy Spirit?

Volume One covers lessons one through five.

Volume Two covers lessons six through eight

Volume Three covers lessons nine through thirteen

BIBLIOGRAPHY
(Books Discussing The Divine Immanence)

We do not by any means recommend all these books — We feel, however, one should be acquainted with the efforts of others in the same area of study.

(1) *Bone of His Bone*, F. J. Huegel, Zondervan Publishing House, 118 pp.

(2) *Some Secrets of Christian Living*, F. B. Meyer, Zondervan Publishing House, 1953, 120 pp.

(3) *How To Live*, G. Campbell Morgan, Parey Jackson, London, England, 1958, 128 pp.

(4) *Born Crucified*, L. E. Maxwell, Moody Press, Chicago, Ill. 1945, 192 pp.

(5) *The Christlike Christian*, Unknown Christian, Zondervan Publishing House, 1962, 144 pp.

(6) *Life in the Spirit*, Mrs. Penn-Lewis, The Overcomer Book Room, 1910, 70 pp.

(7) *The Life of the Spirit*, Hamilton Wright Mabie, Dodd, Mead and Co., 1898, 361 pp.

(8) *The Spirit Filled Life*, John McNeil, Moody Press, 1896, 126 pp.

(9) *Walking in the Spirit*, A.B. Simpson, Christian Publications, Inc., 155 pp.

(10) *His Indwelling Presence*, Norman B. Harrison, Moody Press, 1928, 96 pp.

(11) *The Christ-Life for the Self-Life*, F. B. Meyer, Moody Press, 128 pp.

(12) *Called Unto Holiness*, Ruth Paxton, Moody Press, 1936, 128 pp.

(13) *Like Christ*, Andrew Murray, Prarrie Book Room, 1962, 281 pp.

(14) *The Manhood of the Master*, Harry Emerson Fosdick, Association Press, 1915, 175 pp.

(15) *Lectures to Professing Christians*, Charles G. Finney, Nazarene Publishing House, 1928, 117 pp.

(16) *The Hidden Life*, Charles E. Orr, Gospel Trumphet Co., 1908, 224 pp.

(17) *The Passion For Souls*, J. H. Jowett, Grosset and Dunlap, 1905, 118 pp.

(18) *The Ideal Life,* Henry Drummond, Hodder and Stoughton, 1897, 320 pp.

(19) *Drummond's Addresses,* R. H. Woodward and Co., 1893, 364 pp.

(20) *Crowded To Christ,* L. E. Maxwell, Wm. B. Ferdmans Pub. Co., 1950, 354 pp.

(21) *Discipline and Discovery,* Albert Edward Day, The Disciplined Order of Christ, 1947, 128 pp.

(22) *The Fairest Flower,* F. J. Huegel, Zondervan Publishing House, 1945, 85 pp.

(23) *The Cross and Sanctification,* T. A. Hegre,

(24) *The Divine Conquest,* A. W. Tozer, Revell, 1950.

(25) *Christ Indwelling and Enthroned,* J. O. Sanders, Christian Literature Crusade, 1961.

(26) *Flesh and Spirit,* William Barclay, Abingdon, 1962.

(27) *The Spirit of Life,* Tom Rees.

(28) *God's Provision for Normal Christian Living,* Robert F. Ketcham.

(29) *The Divine Comforter,* J. D. Pentecost.

(30) *The Will of God Your Sanctification,* T. A. Hegre.

(31) *The Spirit of Holiness,* Everett L. Cattell.

(32) *The Power-Full Christian,* An Unknown Christian, Zondervan Publishing House.

(33) *God's Missionary,* Amy Carmichael, Christian Literature Crusade, 1963, 37 pp.

(34) *His Thoughts Said . . . His Father Said . . . ,* Amy Carmichael, Christian Literature Crusade, 1963, 125 pp.

(35) *Kohila,* The Shaping of an Indian Nurse, Amy Carmichael, Christian Literature Crusade, 1956, 183 pp.

(36) *Mimosa,* who was charmed, Amy Carmichael, Christian Literature Crusade, 1963, 162 pp.

(37) *Edges of His Ways,* Amy Carmichael, Christian Literature Crusade, 1955, 197 pp.

(38) *Rose From Brier,* Amy Carmichael, Christian Literature Crusade, 1957, 205 pp.

(39) *Gold Cord,* Amy Carmichael, Christian Literature Crusade, 1957, 375 pp.

(40) *Ploughed Under,* The story of a Little Lover, Amy Carmichael, Christian Literature Crusade, 1953, 155 pp.

CONTENTS

DEDICATION 5

INTRODUCTION 6

BIBLIOGRAPHY 7

Lesson Six
HOW CAN I BE FILLED WITH THE
HOLY SPIRIT? 11

Lesson Seven
HOW CAN I HAVE THE FRUIT OF THE
HOLY SPIRIT? 45

Lesson Eight
HOW CAN THE HOLY SPIRIT HELP ME
TO OVERCOME SIN? 160

Lesson Six

HOW CAN I BE FILLED WITH THE HOLY SPIRIT?

Questions you should answer before you study the lesson.

1. Is Christ living in me? In what manner that gives obvious evidence of the fact?

2. How do we relate to the subject of being filled with the Holy Spirit? Is it optional, imperative, or relative?

3. Do I know anyone of whom I could say, "he is indeed filled with the Holy Spirit?" If so what are the distinctive qualities or virtues of such a person?

4. Am I ever the passive agent in the experience of being filled with the Holy Spirit? If so, when? if not why not?

5. Is the Holy Spirit ever the passive agent in this experience? Specify.

6. Is it possible to lose one's identity in the personality of another person? Please specify who and how.

7. What are the initial and continual elements in being filled with the Holy Spirit? Please use the scripture in your answer.

INTRODUCTION

For more than twenty years I have wanted to write on this subject. In doing so it is my sincere hope that the truth will become a reality in my own heart. I *do* want to become another man — and that man is Christ Jesus. We shall leave no scripture unstudied that in any way relates to this grand theme. We shall not ignore the problems associated. But our primary concern will be with the positive aspects of the subject. We should far rather discover how we *could* be filled with the Holy Spirit than to find out twelve reasons why others were not or could not.

Having just completed five lessons of some 60,000 words on some of the basics of the Holy Spirit, we feel ready to launch into this grandest of all subjects. Perhaps this shall be a long search — it may even be a volume of its own. We shall not cease until we have experimentally arrived in our knowledge of the Divine Immanence.

WHY HAVEN'T WE HEARD MORE ABOUT IT?

When I say "we" I refer to the members of the Restoration Movement. They are much like the disciples at Ephesus — "We did not so much know if there was a Holy Spirit" Cf Acts 19:1-6.

We should answer first of all — and perhaps most of all — *we do not know because we do not know the word of God!* We practice the clergy-laity system, whether we admit it or not. We "go to church" to learn what little we know of the Word of God. Many of our teachers are ill-prepared to instruct us. As a result very little, if any, personal Bible study is done. We are not being critical, for we wish to help. We are only observing a very sad condition.

WHAT IT MEANS TO BE FILLED WITH THE HOLY SPIRIT

It is our understanding that the nature of the Holy Spirit and the nature of Christ are alike — to such an extent that when Jesus said, "he that hath seen me hath seen the Father", He could also have said, "He that hath seen Me hath seen the Holy Spirit". Our Lord was the embodiment of both the Father and the Holy Spirit. This is best indicated in John 14:16-18 — "And I will pray the Father, and He shall give you another Comforter, that he may be with you forever, even the Spirit of truth: whom the world cannot receive for it beholdeth him not; neither knoweth him: *ye know him; for he abideth with you, and shall be in you. I will not leave you desolate: I will come unto you.*"

I John 3:23,24 also teaches this blessed truth: "And this is His commandment, that we should believe in the name of His Son Jesus Christ, and love one another, even as He gave us commandment. And he that keepeth His commandments, abideth in Him, *and He in him. And hereby we know that He abideth in us, by the Spirit which he gave us*".

In the reference in John 14:16-18 notice especially the 17th verse. The one abiding *with* them was to be the same one who would be *in* them. The Holy Spirit had not yet been given at that time, for Christ was not yet glorified. (John 7:38,39). The one who was abiding with them was Christ — He was to request of the Father and He would send them the Holy Spirit; (which was fulfilled on Pentecost). When this took place Christ would be in them through His representative the Holy Spirit.

12

How Can I Be Filled With the Holy Spirit?

It would seem John's epistle in 3:23,24 is a commentary on his gospel reference of John 14:16-18. To be filled with the Holy Spirit is to be filled with Christ. To be filled with Christ is to be filled with the Holy Spirit. How shall we be filled with Christ? How can we make this inward substitution? All we know about Christ is found in the four gospels. The reason we are not more like Christ is because we do not know more about Him — and what we do know about Him we fail to apply to life. It shall be our purpose to so digest the life of our Lord as to make His life our life. The personal application of the gospel record accompanied by prayer and a holy honesty shall be our pursuit.

"But we all, with unveiled face beholding as in a mirror, the glory of the Lord, are transformed into the same image from glory to glory, even as from the Lord the Spirit" II Cor. 3:18.

Aaron, Aaron, make us a god to go before us — as for this man Moses who led us out of the land of Egypt — we know not what has become of him. (Acts 7:40). But *we* know what had become of him. For forty days Moses stood with "unveiled face" in the presence of the great God Jehovah. When after forty days he came down he had a glow on his face so intense he had to put a veil over his face to protect the eyes of those who might see him — (or was the veil there to hide the sad fact of the gradual dissipation of the glow of God?) The point is the same — Paul is saying in his second letter to the "saints" at Corinth what happened to Moses physically should happen to us spiritually. What happened to Moses on the outside should happen to us on the inside. The "glory of God" wonderfully changed the appearance of Moses. The glory of God is to just as wonderfully change our inward (and outward) appearance. But how is this glorious transformation produced? *By the simple procedure of looking with unveiled face into the mirror.* What is the mirror?

We believe James 1:23-25 answers the question: "For if any one is a hearer of the word and not a doer, he is like unto a man beholding his natural face *in a mirror:* for he beholdeth himself, and goeth away, and straightway forgetteth what manner of man he was. But he that looketh into the perfect law, the law of liberty, and so continueth, being not a hearer that forgetteth but a doer that worketh, this man shall be blessed in his doing".

What do we see in the mirror? i.e. what do we see in the word of the Lord? — The text says we behold *"the glory of the Lord"* — Please do not stumble over the word "glory" — we can use the word "character" or "nature" as a synonym — Let's read the text with this change: "But we all with unveiled face beholding as in a mirror the character of the Lord are transformed into the same image from character to character even as from the Lord the Spirit" II Cor. 3:18.

The gospel accounts were written through the direction of the Holy Spirit for the express purpose of revealing the character of God as seen in the person of Jesus His Son.

There are two important words in this text — they are: *beholding* and *unveiled*. The word *beholding* is much stronger than mere *looking* or *observing* — *contemplating* or *meditating* would be much closer. This is a word indicating a penetration or insight — *looking into*, would carry the thought — This then must be the manner or attitude used when looking into the mirror — behold with the enlightened eyes of your understanding or heart. No casual observation will ever produce the transformation here promised. The vision of Saul on the Damascus road — to behold until he saw nothing else — indeed until he could see nothing else — to look until the image is stamped indelibly on the inner consciousness. To behold and wonder until everyone and everything else fades from sight and we behold Jesus only.

But such a penetration can never be made until the veil (or veils) have been removed — and we with *unveiled face* behold the character of the Lord. The Jews had a veil over their eyes which altogether held the true character of Jesus from them — this veil was obedience to the law as a method of justification with God. Until this veil was taken away they were lost — lost from the grace of God in His Son — lost from the power of His Son through His blood — lost to the beauty of Holy Spirit produced holiness. Many of us are lost in the same manner. We have veils over our eyes — we cannot but very dimly see the glory or character of the Lord; our fleeting and vague views of Him have but little effect upon our character.

Let us have a look at another verse that discusses this same concept in a different figure of speech:

"But *put ye on* the Lord Jesus Christ and make not provision for the flesh to fulfil the lusts thereof" Romans 13:14.

The expression *"put ye on"* is from the language of the theatre and refers to putting on a character as an actor would "get into character". Of course the emphasis is much stronger — we are to lose our identity in the one we portray. We are to indeed be "even as He was in this world" — to walk as He walked to be the "body of Christ". Paul expressed it in the word of Galations 2:20 " . . . it is no longer I who live but Christ who liveth in me . . ." or in Philippians 2:5 "Have this mind in you which was in Christ Jesus" — or the expression "we have the mind of Christ" as expressed in Philippians 4:2 " . . . to be of the same mind in the Lord".

If I ever believed anything I believe it is possible — yea God's will — that we become another man — we can so learn of Him — so imbibe His Spirit — so allow Him to live in us through His indwelling by His representative the Holy Spirit, that we will lose our identity in His identity.

This is no mystery—there are any number of actors or actresses who testify by their experience — to say nothing of their performance — that they have so subjugated their own personalities in identifying themselves with the character portrayed that they have had great difficulty in reidentifying themselves. What a shame that we have not so learned Christ! When will we so behold Him — so learn of Him — so put Him on? How many actors have memorized a script longer than the gospel of Luke in order to act out for ninety minutes the life and words of a fictional or historical person? — the script was so well known as to become a veritable part of the person portraying it — why have we so miserably failed in our participation in Christ? We are not called on to *ham act* a few lines we have only half learned — we are called on to share in the Divine Nature. We are to walk as He walked. Why do we fail? *The answer is in the unveiled face — What are some of the veils we must remove before we can behold His Glory in such a manner as to be transformed into the same image?* (We might add that such veils must constantly be removed — it is a continuing action.)

15

There are many of them — here are only the ones I have found veiling my vision —

1. The veil of willful ignorance of the character of Christ.
2. The veil of body (belly) worship.
3. The veil of the lust of the flesh.
4. The veil of pride.
5. The veil of selfishness.
6. The veil of worry.
7. The veil of resentment.
8. The veil of self-centeredness.
9. The veil of oversensitiveness.
10. The veil of undisciplined mind.
11. The veil of covetousness.
12. The veil of boredom.
13. The veil of envy or jealousy.
14. The veil of irritation with little things.
15. The veil of self-justification.

There may be others — I am sure you can define and discover the veils peculiar to you — perhaps you share my concern in obtaining an unveiled view of Him whose presence and person beheld in all His beauty will give us the power to transform ourselves by His Spirit into His own image.

Shall we fearlessly find these veils and tear them from our view of Him?

THE VEIL OF WILLFUL IGNORANCE AND ITS REMOVAL:

Why are we willfully ignorant? Please do not multiply your sin by saying we are not willfully ignorant.

We are! But why? Why do we neglect the study of the life of our Lord? Why do we fail to memorize one verse each day or each week? Surely we could, and should memorize one verse of the beautiful gospel each week — but we do not do it — Why? We could blame it on original sin or the Adamic nature — perhaps this is so — but no one *must* be willfully ignorant — we are reticent to work also — but we do not often and continually absent ourselves from our jobs — we must eat so we work. A sense of necessity produces the basic motive for much of our action. As sincere believers we heard of the need and necessity of giving some of our money to the Lord's work — so we give it.

How Can I Be Filled With the Holy Spirit?

We have heard of the need for church attendance so we attend. We have heard Jesus say — "I was sick and ye visited me" — and we do call on the sick.

The authority of God and Christ and our sense of obligation to them underlies all our action in any realm. Do we have divine authority for being filled with the Holy Spirit? Read it: "Be not drunken with wine, wherein is riot but be filled with the Spirit", Ephesians 5:18.

If deacon Jones came into the meeting house staggering under the influence of wine we would really become concerned because God said "be not drunken with wine". What indication do we have that the same deacon Jones is filled with the Spirit? We remember when the very first deacons were chosen they were to be "filled with the Spirit" — read Acts 6:3-5 for yourself — "Look ye out therefore, brethren, from among you seven men of good report, *full of the Spirit* and of wisdom..." And the saying pleased the whole multitude: and they *chose Stephen, a man full of faith and of the Holy Spirit* ...

We are willfully negligent because we have forgotten the absolute necessity of being filled with the Holy Spirit. It is as much of a command to be filled with the Spiirt as it is not to be drunk! We are all under the same obligation to obey one command as we are to obey the other. When we obtain a conscience on this subject we will begin to move in the right direction — Until this happens nothing will happen. Do you now believe God wants every Christian to be filled with the Holy Spirit? Please read Acts 13:52 in this connection. "And the disciples were filled with joy *and with the Holy Spirit*".

What more do we need to break out of our apathy?

Has this helped you to remove the veil?

Will you by the aid of the Holy Spirit no longer remain willfully negligent and ignorant of this glorious subject?

To aid you in your removal of this veil from your eyes will you here and now sign your name to this statement?

I, _____ _____ "my conscience bearing witness with me in the Holy Spirit" (Romans 9:1) do hereby promise God and the lost world in which I live, and the body of Christ of which I am a member that beginning today I will no longer willfully neglect this great area of blessing through

Bible study, but will beginning right now do everything I can to be filled with the Holy Spirit, signed: ....
If you do not like to sign statements work out some better way to tear away the veil — but we had better do something definite if not drastic in the removal of willful neglect and ignorance. Without its removal we cannot even begin to move for Christ.

THE REMOVAL OF THE VEIL OF BODY WORSHIP:
"Whose God is their belly" . . . Phil. 3:19.

We cannot emphasize too strongly that the removal of these veils is a continuing process. There is a fight between the flesh and the Spirit as long as we live in this fleshly body. " . . . for the two are contrary to each other, that you may not do the things that ye would". (Gal. 5:16). "His ye are whom ye serve.. " (Rom. 6:16). Why will men choose to serve the flesh? Why make the desires of the body their God? There must indeed be some encouragement apart from man — "To will is present — but to do that which is good is not — When will we believe Paul when he said — "I know that in my flesh dwelleth no good thing!" America is pre-conditioned and brain-washed in the area of fleshly indulgence and body worship.

Samuel Rutherford has well stated the case:

"What was the hook that took David and snared him first in adultery, but his self-lust? and then in murder, but his self-credit and self-esteem? What led Peter on to deny his Lord? Was it not a piece of himself, and self-love to a whole skin? What made Judas sell his Master for thirty pieces of silver, but the *idolizing and avaricious self?* What made Demas go off the way of the Gospel to embrace the present world? Even *self-love* and a love of gain for himself. Every man blameth the devil for his sins; but the great devil, the house devil of every man, the house devil that eateth and lieth in every bosom, is the idol that killeth all, himself (his body or his belly). Oh! blessed are they who can deny themselves, and put on Christ in the room of themselves! O sweet word: "I live no more but Christ liveth in me". (Quoted by Mantle in *The Way of the Cross* and by Maxwell in *Crowded to Christ*). We shall never see Christ until through fasting and prayer this veil is painfully torn from the eyes of our heart. Self-indulgence — self-worship (represented by the word "belly") cannot be crucified without prayer and fasting. We somehow imagine there must be some form of painless crucifixion for the flesh and we can deny ourselves and it won't hurt a bit! This is the idle dream of the belly worshipper who does not come to see past the veil of the flesh.

They who are thus satisfied cannot please God. They cannot be like Christ; they cannot be His disciples or learners. They will not tear away the covering for their first look at Him — when we will not deny ourselves we cannot even *begin* to learn of Him.

THE REMOVAL OF THE VEIL OF THE LUST OF THE FLESH

"Wherefore *in all things it behoved him to be made like unto his brethren,* that he might be a merciful and faithful high priest in things pertaining to God, to make reconciliation for the sins of the people. For *in that he himself hath suffered being tempted,* he is able to succour them that are tempted." (Hebrews 2:17,18).

"For we have not an high priest which cannot be touched with the feeling of our infirmities but was *in all points tempted like as we are,* yet without sin. Let us therefore come boldy unto the throne of grace, that we may obtain mercy, and find grace to help in time of need." (Hebrews 4:15,16).

Are you ever tempted to simply give up and quit in this battle with desire? Not give in or give up to evil desire, for we do that often enough; indeed such yielding becomes the reason for this larger and darker temptation — to simply quit the fight — to drop out of the race — to forget the Faith? Please look again — "You cannot imagine joy as a virtue except in the presence of the temptation to be discouraged." It is equally true — you cannot imagine purity of thought as a virtue except in the presence of the temptation to be impure and inwardly an adulterer.

"No, when the fight begins with himself, a man's worth something. God stoops o'er His head, Satan looks up between his feet — both tug — He's left himself in the middle: the soul wakes and grows."

All virtue is a positive quality attained through struggle — sometime through "strong crying and many tears". (Heb. 5:7).

Please notice our use of the word "desire" in the place of "lust". We could more accurately say "strong desire". We are all filled with desire — indeed man seems to be best characterized as "one big desire". We have the marvelous privilege of choosing the area where this capacity will be exercised. We can take this God-given capacity into whatever area we choose. There are three areas where Satan lives. Three areas given over exclusively to his control. They are:

(1) Flesh — *all* illicit sexual relationships.
(2) Eyes — *all* illicit use of possessions.
(3) Pride — *all* illicit appeal to the ego.

We have a "built-in" capacity to want — to desire — to lust — how we use it is the ONE big problem of man. When we think again on the three realms mentioned above we wonder what area is left when we have considered these three — ? There is a proper use for the attraction of the opposite sex to man's desire. There is a right use of possessions as related to man's desire. This is also true in the desire to exercise our individual capacities or the development of the ego. When we have lived properly with the opposite sex, when we have used our possessions as we should, when we have thought of ourselves as we ought — what is left to consider?

The problem then is ONLY with *how* we shall use the capacity God has given us — the capacity to *want* with intensity. We could profitably consider the two other areas, i.e. (1) possessions, and (2) ego, but we are concerned here with "the flesh". There are a number of observations we have gleaned from scripture and experience. These have helped in the removal of this veil. (Please remember — it is a continuing work).

(1) Look at your body! Look at your arm — your foot — your face. Take hold of yourself — you are flesh and bone. Please remember the body is *one* — the flesh is *one* — all the desires of the body are very closely allied — if not integrated. Therefore to control or limit one expression of the body affects all other expressions of the body. As example — go on an extended fast — thus limiting and controlling the expression of eating — and see how you have also limited the desire for the opposite sex. Another natural (or God-given) need or desire of the body is for warmth — place your body in an extended period of bitter cold and tell me how strong your desires are for the opposite sex? — or even for food? A natural expression of the body is the expending of energy — work at hard manual labor for 12 hours and notice the difference in the desire for the opposite sex.

What is the point here? A *very, very important one!*

I hear someone say — "I simply cannot overcome the lust of the flesh - the desire is beyond my control". Wait a minute—can you go on a fast? Can you control the expending of your energy? *When you think you cannot control the body or the flesh in one area you can in another. —since the body is one you thus can control it in every area.* We should say above and beyond all we have said that without Christ we will not *want* to control our bodies — without His indwelling presence we will have no reason to "buffet our bodies and bring them into subjection". We pre-suppose that you are all earnest Christians with a deep desire to tear away the veil of the lust of the flesh.

(2) All desires of the flesh are aroused, and to a large extent controlled, by stimuli. We all know the appeal to the desires of the flesh are through the five senses of: (1) sight; (2) sound; (3) taste; (4) touch ;(5) smelling. How greatly increased is our desire for food when related to sight or smell, or even sound. This is surely obvious when related to the matter of sexual desire. Please, please recognize that you *can* choose to limit or eliminate the stimuli of sexual desire. You cannot sit in front of a T.V. set and watch the sensual movements of scantily clad women and not be sexually aroused—not unless you are on an extended fast—in such a case the desire will be there but greatly lessened by the effects of your fast (please notice the interpretation of these two thoughts). You cannot leaf through the pages of a pornographic magazine and ignore the stimuli. You *can* refuse to look at such a program on T.V. You *can* refuse to pick up such a magazine. But once again—you must have the consuming desire to see Him —to see Him without the veil of illicit sexual desire. We cannot and will not see Him until we do so without this veil!

We shall consider one more veil and its removal—we could become so concerned with the veils that we have no time or desire left to look at Him. We ask you to identify and tear away whatever veil hides His face from you.

THE REMOVAL OF THE VEIL OF PRIDE

Of all four of the veils we are to consider—i.e.: (1) The Veil of willful ignorance of the character of Christ; (2) Body worship; (3) The lust of the flesh; (4) The veil of pride—surely

21

this last is the most insidious. Preachers and teachers should be able to speak with authority and experience concerning this veil.

Let me speak out of my heart—and out of my own need on this subject:

First of all, how incredible it is that we should have pride or "vainglory" in anything! The question of Paul to the Corinthians comes with real force to my heart —"And what hast thou which thou didst not receive . . . why dost thou glory?" (I Cor. 4:7). But somehow we imagine God's gifts are our private possessions. The plain fact of the matter is we are struggling with the problem of pride and have *not* overcome it. What then shall we say? We shall say "have this mind in you which was also in Christ Jesus" and we will have no pride. Please note the context in which the above quotation occurs: Phil. 2:5-11—"Have this mind in you, which was also in Christ Jesus: who, existing in the form of God, *counted* not the being on an equality with God a thing to be grasped, but *emptied* himself, *taking* the form of a servant, being made in the likeness of men; . . .". Please notice that Jesus had much - was indeed rich —"He need not have been born in a manger, lived in a laborer's home in a despised town, attended a village school, earned His living by the sweat of His face. *He deliberately chose* the lowliest place that He might evidence the attitude of mind He expected in His disciples." *(J. Oswald Sanders).*

If we wait until we feel humble-minded about everything before we manifest in our actions and works our humility, we will usually just wait—and when we do feel very humble about something - it is usually only an expression of our humiliation and a period of recuperation for our injured ego. We must be like our Lord and deliberately *choose* to take the lowly place—deliberately choose to serve instead of being served. Here are some searching questions that have helped me to choose to empty myself.

1. Is there a place in my life where I am ashamed of Jesus Christ?
2. Do I still feel the thrill of the miraculous when I meditate on God?
3. Have I no vision because of my own too close calculations?
4. Have I been delivered from fear of failure?

5. Am I aware that fear and laziness are as sinful as greed and ambition?
6. Is the symbol of my prayer the open hand or the open heart?
7. Am I worn out through interior tensions and excitements?
8. Am I just drifting?
9. Is Christ's love for men my very pulse?
10. Am I so satisfied with Jesus Christ that my life has His charm about it?
11. Are my prejudices very appealing to me?
12. Do I have my money, or does my money have me?
13. Is negative thinking one of my sins?
14. Is my criticism of others constructive, or merely defensive?
15. Am I the same person to all the people I meet?
16. Is a postponed restitution the block in my spiritual growth?
17. Is my boldness blind?
18. Have I forgotten how to be sorry?
19. Does the lust for other things choke all that God puts in?
20. How long do I nurse a grouch?
21. Will I let the last conceit go, i.e. that I know myself?
22. Have I refused to attend the funeral of my own independence?
23. Am I a museum specimen for God, or a useful Christian?
24. Has egoism and egotism made God seem unreal to me?
25. Have I originality and Christian Charm?
26. Do I unreservedly believe the life of faith is the most secure life?
27. Am I more devoted to a cause, or a group, than I am to Jesus Christ?
28. Am I aware of the power and value of a few minutes of silence?
29. Am I ignorant of what God can do with my capabilities?
30. Do I work for God or does God work through me?

We have only spoken of four of the fifteen veils — please identify each one of them for yourself — but our purpose is not to delineate the problem but to offer the answer. It is found in seeing Him with an unveiled face. Shall we attempt it?

What would happen if we were to spend three and one-half years following Jesus through the gospels as the twelve spent the same time following Him through Galilee and Judea? If we spent as much time during these three and one-half years as we imagine the disciples spent — i.e. in reading, memorizing, and meditating on the gospel accounts — if we attempted during this period of time to take Christ into every circumstance of life — even as did the twelve - I wonder what would happen? Would we not learn of Him and be like Him? Would not this enable the Holy Spirit within our bodies to fill our lives? Would this be the experience of which we speak and seek called "being filled with the Holy Spirit?"

To make this much more than an idle - or idealistic dream - let's walk with Him through one day as it relates to just one part of His life. Let's go to the stable with the Bethlehem shepherds — but we must go there not from the hills of Bethlehem but from our own bedroom. Please read again - just as if you had never read it before - the accounts in Luke 2:1-20. Verse 20 says: "And the shepherds returned glorifying and praising God *for all the things that they had heard and seen,* even as it was spoken unto them". For what were they glorifying and praising God? What lessons did they learn from their experience? What did they learn of Jesus that would help them to be like Him? Obviously they must have wondered greatly that their Messian would be born in a stable! A very pointed lesson in humility was taught when He emptied Himself and chose such a lowly place for His beginning on earth. Here are some questions that they might have asked that will perhaps bring into focus the example of our Lord as found in His birth.

1. *If the king of the Jews chose to be born in a stable, of what do I as a Jew have to be proud?* Should I not be humble-minded as a subject of such a humble king? This question is to you and me. What a demonic quality is pride. Why should we feel we have possession of anything? Remember - Jesus *chose* to leave heaven and share the humiliation of humanity - and He did it willingly - even joyfully!

2. *Must there not be hope for the humblest man on earth since the anointed of God can be born in a stable?* God loves the acknowledgment of Himself as the creator and Provider. None need feel rejected and unworthy. This was the treatment of His Son - and yet He was approved and beloved of the Father.

3. *This life must be but the beginning of God's purpose for man — does He not provide more for the cattle of the field than He has provided for His own Son?* How can we place our satisfaction and hopes in the context of material possessions when God and the Messiah regard them so lightly?

Here are some questions for you and me as we attempt to be like Him in this one day of life:

1. Will I meet with the Shepherds this morning at His stable to worship Him - or am I sufficient unto myself without a time of devotion before Him? You must choose!

2. How humble-minded am I before breakfast? Remember - we can *choose* to humble-minded!

3. Am I addicted to coffee to such an extent that my temperament is controlled by drinking or not drinking? Is the kingdom of God now dependent on the drinking of coffee? (Remember "the Kigdom of God" is the rule of God in the heart of man.)

4. How do I react to irritation and interruption? Where is your lowli-mindedness now? *When* do you plan on counting the other person better than yourself? Most especially when the other person is your wife or children?

5. Are you going to stand up and fight for your "rights" today — remember Jesus had many rights He did not claim by force. Right is in the hands of God — our part is love and service. God will finally repay — he was meek (not weak) and lowly in heart - so as must we be - so must we *choose* to be! Please remember the promised aid of the Holy Spirit in strengthening by His power our inward man. It is thus we are filled with the Holy Spirit. He can help if we choose to do His will. It is only when we decide on the side of humility that we can expect the aid of the Holy Spirit "put to death the deeds of the body". When we *do* choose to not revile when we are reviled we can then claim and experience the aid of the Holy Spirit in enabling us to let Christ dwell in us — and express His love through us. The more often we do this — the more completely we yield to His will in all the areas of our daily living, the more fully and completely we are "filled with the Holy Spirit".

6. How will you feel this morning when you see that fellow you "simply cannot stand" (there are some people who are always

saying the wrong thing and rubbing you the wrong way). Did Jesus associate (or even work with any loathsome persons?). Jesus prayed for His enemies and asked us to do the same — please, please — commit the man (or woman) to the Lord — and quit taking God's place as judge. Although he is obviously condemned — you arouse resentment because you take God's place of judgment—commit him to God and *choose* to be humbleminded.

What would happen if we were to follow our Lord throughout the gospel accounts and make application of those qualities of character wherever we found them? If we did this every day for three and one-half years, we would become so personally acquainted with Him that soon - in deed and truth it would "be no longer I that live but Christ that liveth in me", (but not without a crucifixion of self). It can be done - do you know of a higher or holier pursuit? Is there a greater need in the church today?

His command — and our privilege — still stands — ". . . be filled with the Spirit". (Eph. 5:18).

Here is a chapter from a book by Henry Drummond *(Address By Drummond)* which has helped me in understanding this grand subject — please read it carefully.

THE FORMULA OF SANCTIFICATION

A formula, a receipt, for Sanctification - can one seriously speak of this mighty change as if the process were as definite as for the production of so many volts of electricity? It is impossible to doubt it. Shall a mechanical experiment succeed infallibly, and the one vital experiment of humanity remain a chance? Is corn to grow by method, and character by caprice? If we cannot calculate to a certainty that the forces of religion will do their work, then is religion vain. And if we cannot express the law of these forces in simple words, then is Christianity not the world's religion, but the world's conundrum.

Where, then, shall one look for such a formula? Where one would look for any formula - among the text-books. And if we turn to the textbooks of Christianity we shall find a formula for this problem as clear and precise as any in the mechanical sciences. If this simple rule, moreover, be but followed fearlessly, it will yield the result of a perfect character as surely as any result that is guaranteed by the laws of nature. The finest expression of this rule in Scripture, or indeed in any literature, is probably one drawn up and condensed into a single verse by Paul. You will find it in a letter - the second to the Corinthians - written by him to some Christian people who, in a city which was a byword for depravity and licentiousness, were seeking the higher life. To see the point of the words we must take them from the immensely improved rendering of the Revised translation for the older Version in this case greatly obscures the sense. They are these: "We all, with unveiled face reflecting as a mirror the glory of the Lord, are transformed into the same image from glory to glory, even as from the Lord the Spirit."

Now observe at the outset the entire contradiction of all our previous efforts, in the simple passive "we *are* transformed." We *are changed,* as the Old Version has it - we do not change ourselves. No man can change himself. Throughout the New Testament you will find that wherever these moral and spiritual transformations are described the verbs are in the passive. Presently it will be pointed out that there is a *rationale* in this; but meantime do not toss these words aside as if this passivity denied all human effort or ignored intelligible law. What is implied for the soul here is no more than is everywhere claimed for the body. In physiology the verbs describing the processes of growth are in the passive. Growth is not voluntary; it takes place, it happens, it is wrought upon matter. So here. "Ye must be born again" - we cannot born ourselves. "Be not conformed to this world, but *be ye transformed*" - we are subjects to transforming influence, we do not transform ourselves. Not more certain is it that it is something outside the thermometer that produces a change in the thermometer, than it is something outside the soul of man that produces a moral change upon him. That he must be susceptible to that change, that he must be a party to it, goes without saying; but that neither his aptitude nor his will can produce it, is equally certain.

Obvious as it ought to seem, this may be to some an almost startling revelation. The change we have been striving after is not to be produced by any more striving after. It is to be wrought upon us by the moulding of hands beyond our own. As the branch ascends, and the bud bursts, and the fruit reddens under the co-operation of influences from the outside air, so man rises to the higher stature under invisible pressures from without. The radical defect of all our former methods of sanctification was the attempt to generate from within that which can only be wrought upon us from without. According to the first Law of Motion: Every body continues in its state of rest, or of uniform motion in a straight line, except in so far as it may be compelled *by impressed forces* to change that state. This is also a first law of Christianity. Every man's character remains as it is, or continues in the direction in which it is going, until it is compelled *by impressed forces* to change that state. Our failure has been the failure to put ourselves in the way of the impressed forces. There is a clay, and there is a Potter; we have tried to be the clay and to mould the clay.

Whence, then, these pressures, and where this Potter? The answer of the formula is "By reflecting as a mirror the glory of the Lord we are changed." But this is not very clear. What is the "glory" of the Lord, and how can mortal man reflect it, and how can that act as an "impressed force" in moulding him to a nobler form? The word "glory' — the word which has to bear the weight of holding those "impressed forces" - is a stranger in current speech, and our first duty is to seek out its equivalent in working English. It suggests at first a radiance of some kind, something dazzling or glittering, some halo such as the old masters loved to paint round the heads of their Ecce Homos. But that is paint, mere matter, the visible symbol of some unseen thing. What is that unseen thing? It is that of all unseen things the most radiant, the most beautiful, the most Divine, and that is *Character.* On earth, in Heaven, there is nothing so great, so glorious as this. The word has many meanings; in ethics it can have but one. Glory is character, and nothing less, and it can be nothing more. The earth is 'full of the glory of the Lord," because it is full of His character. The "Beauty of the Lord" is character: "The effulgence of His Glory" is character. "The Glory of the Only Begotten" is character, the character which is "fulness of grace and truth". And when God told His people *His*

28

name He simply gave them His character, His character which was Himself: "And the Lord proclaimed the name of the Lord . . . the Lord, the Lord God, merciful and gracious, long-suffering and abundant in goodness and truth." Glory then is not something intangible, or ghostly, or transcendental. If it were this how could Paul ask men to reflect it? Stripped of its physical and enswathement it is Beauty, moral and spiritual Beauty, Beauty infinitely real, infinitely exalted, yet infinitely near and infinitely communicable.

With this explanation read over the sentence once more in paraphrase: We all reflecting as a mirror the character of Christ are transformed into the same Image from character to character - from a poor character to a better one, from a better one to one a little better still, from that to one still more complete, until by slow degrees the Perfect Image is attained. Here the solution of the problem of sanctification is compressed into a sentence: Reflect the character of Christ, and you will become like Christ.

All men are mirrors—that is the first law on which this formula is based. One of the aptest descriptions of a human being is that he is a mirror. As we sat at table to-night the world in which each of us lived and moved througout this day was focussed in the room. What we saw as we looked at one another was not one another, but one another's world. We were an arrangement of mirrors. The scenes we saw were all reproduced; the people we met walked to and fro; they spoke, they bowed, they passed us by, did everything over again as if it had been real. When we talked, we were but looking at our own mirror and describing what flitted across it; our listening was not hearing, but seeing - we but looked on our neighbor's mirror. All human intercourse is a seeing of reflections. I meet a stranger in a railway carriage. The cadence of his first word tells me he is English, and comes from Yorkshire. Without knowing it he has reflected his birthplace, his parents, and the long history of their race. Even physiologically he is a mirror. His second sentence records that he is a politician, and a faint inflexion in the way he pronounces *The Times* reveals his party. In his next remarks I see reflected a whole world of experiences. The books he has read, the people he has met, the influences that have played upon him and made him the man he is - these are all registered there by a pen which lets nothing pass, and whose writing can never be blotted out. What I am reading in him meantime he also reading in me; and before the journey is over we could half write each other's lives. Whether we like it or not, we live in glass houses. The mind, the memory, the soul, is simply a vast chamber panelled with looking-glass. And upon this miraculous arrangement and endowment depends the capacity of mortal souls to "reflect the character of the Lord."

But this is not all. If all these varied reflections from our so-called secret life are patent to the world, how close the writing, how complete the record, within the soul itself? For the influences we meet are not simply held for a moment on the polished surface and thrown off again into space. Each is retained where first it fell, and stored up in the soul for ever.

This law of Assimilation is the second, and by far the most impressive truth which underlies the formula of sanctification - the truth that men are not only mirrors, but that these mirrors, so far from being mere reflectors of the fleeting things they see, transfer into their own inmost substance, and hold in permanent preservation, the things that they reflect. No one knows how the soul can hold these things. No one knows how the miracle is done. No phenomenon in nature, no process in chemistry, no chapter in necromancy can ever help us begin to understand this amazing operation. For, think of it, the past is not only focussed there, in a man's soul, it is there. How could it be reflected from there if it were not there? All things that he has ever seen, known, felt, believed of the surrounding world are now within him, have become part of him, in part are him - he has been changed into their image. He may deny it, he may resent it, but they are there. They do not adhere to him, they are transfused through him. He cannot alter or rub them out. They are not in his memory, they are in him. His soul is as they have filled it, made it, left it. These things, these books, these events, these influences are his makers. In their hands are life and death, beauty, and deformity. When once the image or likeness of any of these is fairly presented to the soul, no power on earth can hinder two things happening - it must be absorbed into the soul, and forever reflected back again from character.

Upon these astounding yet perfectly obvious psychological facts, Paul bases his doctrine of sanctification. He sees that character is a thing built up by slow degress, that it is hourly changing for better or for worse according to the images which flit across it. One step further and the whole length and breadth of the application of these ideas to the central problem of religion will stand before us.

THE ALCHEMY OF INFLUENCE

If events change men, much more persons. No man can meet another on the street without making some mark upon him. We say we exchange words when we meet; what we exchange is souls. And when intercourse is very close and very frequent, so complete is this exchange that recognizable bits of the one soul begin to show in the other's nature, and the second is conscious of a similar and growing debt to the first.

This mysterious approximating of two souls who has not witnessed? Who has not watched some old couple come down life's pilgrimage hand in hand, with such gentle trust and joy in one another that their very faces wore the self-same look? These were not two souls; it was a composite soul. It did not matter to which of the two you spoke you would have said the same words to either. It was quite indifferent which replied, each would have said the same. Half a century's *reflecting* had told upon them; they were changed into the same image. It is the Law of Influence that *we become like those whom we habitually admire:* these had become alike because they habitually admired. Through all the range of literature, of history, and biography this law presides. Men are all mosaics of other men. There was a savor of David about Jonathan and a savor of Jonathan about David. Jean Valjean, in the masterpiece of Victor Hugo, is Bishop Bienvenu risen from the dead. Metempsychosis is a fact. George Eliot's message to the world was that men and women make men and women The Family, the cradle of mankind, has no meaning apart from this. Society itself is nothing but a rallying point for these omnipotent forces to do their work. On the doctrine of Influence, in short, the whole vast pyramid of humanity is built.

But it was reserved for Paul to make the supreme application of the Law of Influence. It was a tremendous inference to make, but he never hesitated. He himself was a changed man; he knew exactly what had done it; it was Christ. On the Damascus road

31

they met, and from that hour his life was absorbed in His. The effect could not but follow—on words, on deeds, on career, on creed. The "impressed forces" did their vital work. He became like Him Whom he habitually loved. "So we all," he writes, "reflecting as a mirror the glory of Christ, are changed into the same image."

Nothing could be more simple, more intelligible, more natural, more supernatural. It is an analogy from an every-day fact. Since we are what we are by the impacts of those who surround us, those who surround themselves with the highest will be those who change into the highest. There are some men and some women in whose company we are always at our best. While with them we cannot think mean thoughts or speak ungenerous words. Their mere presence is elevation, purification, sanctity. All the best stops in our nature are drawn out by their intercourse, and we find a music in our souls that was never there before. Suppose even *that* influence prolonged through a month, a year, a lifetime, and what could not life become? Here, even on the common plane of life, talking our language, walking our streets, working side by side, are sanctifiers of souls; here, breathing through common clay, is Heaven; here, energies charged even through a temporal medium with the virtue of regeneration. If to live with men, diluted to the millionth degree with the virtue of the Highest, can exalt and purify the nature, what bounds can be set to the influence of Christ? To live with Socrates—with unveiled face— must have made one wise; with Aristides, just. Francis of Assisi must have made one gentle; Savonarola, strong. But to have lived with Christ must have made one like Christ; that is to say, *A Christian.*

As a matter of fact, to live with Christ did produce this effect. It produced it in the case of Paul. And during Christ's lifetime the experiment was tried in an even more startling form. A few raw, unspiritual, uninspiring men, were admitted to the inner circle of His friendship. The change began at once. Day by day we can almost see the first disciples grow. First there steals over them the faintest possible adumbration of His character, and occasionally, very occasionally, they do a thing or say a thing that they could not have done or said had they not been living there. Slowly the spell of His Life deepens. Reach after reach of their nature is overtaken, thawed, subjugated, sanctified. Their manner softens, their words become more gentle, their conduct more unselfish. As swallows who have found a summer, as frozen buds the spring, their starved humanity bursts into a fuller life. They do not know how it is, but they are different men. One day they find themselves like their Master, going about and doing good. To themselves it is unaccountable, but they cannot do otherwise. They were not told to do it, it came to them to do it. But the people who watch them know well how to account for it—"They have been," they whisper, "with Jesus." Already even, the mark and seal of His character is upon them—"They have been with Jesus." Unparalleled phenomenon, that these poor fishermen should remind other men of Christ! Stupendous victory and mystery of regeneration that mortal men should suggest to the world, *God!*

There is something almost melting in the way His contemporaries, and John especially, speak of the influence of Christ. John lived himself in daily wonder at Him; he was over-powered, over-awed, entranced, transfigured. To his mind it was impossible for anyone to come under this influence and ever be the same again. "Whosoever abideth in Him sinneth not," he said. It was inconceivable that he should sin, as inconceivable as that ice should live in a burning sun, or darkness co-exist with noon. If anyone did sin, it was to John the simple proof that he could never have met Christ. "Whosoever sinneth," he exclaims, "hath not seen *Him,* neither knows *Him.*" Sin was abashed in this Presence. Its roots withered. Its sway and victory were for ever at an end.

But these were His contemporaries. It was easy for *them* to be influenced by Him, for they were every day and all the day together. But how can we mirror that which we have never seen? How can all this stupendous result be produced by a Memory, by the scantiest of all Biographies, by One who lived and left this earth eighteen hundred years ago? How can modern men today make Christ, the absent Christ, their most constant companion still? The answer is that Friendship is a spiritual thing. It is independent of Matter, or Space, or Time. That which I love in my friend is not that which I see. What

influences me in my friend is not his body but his spirit. It
would have been an ineffable experience truly to have lived at
that time—

> "I think when I read the sweet story of old
>> How when Jesus was here among men,
> He took little children like lambs to his fold,
>> I should like to have been with Him then.
> I wish that His hand had been laid on my head,
>> That his arms had been thrown around me,
> And that I had seen His kind look when he said,
>> 'Let the little ones come unto me'."

And yet, if Christ were to come into the world again few of us
probably would ever have a chance of seeing Him. Millions of
her subjects, in this little country, have never seen their own
Queen. And there would be millions of the subjects of Christ
who could never get within speaking distance of Him if He
were here. Our companionship with Him, like all true companionship, is a spiritual communion. All friendship, all love,
human and Divine, is purely spiritual. It was after He was risen
that He influenced even the disciples most. Hence in reflecting
the character of Christ, it is no real obstacle that we may never
have been in visible contact with Himself.

There lived once a young girl whose perfect grace of character was the wonder of those who knew her. She wore on her
neck a gold locket which no one was ever allowed to open.
One day, in a moment of unusual confidence, one of her companions was allowed to touch its spring and learn its secret.
She saw written these words—*"Whom having not seen, I love."*
That was the secret of her beautiful life. She had been changed
into the Same Image.

Now this is not imitation, but a much deeper thing. Mark
this distinction. For the difference in the process, as well as in
the result, may be as great as that between a photograph secured
by the infallible pencil of the sun, and the rude outline from a
school-boy's chalk. Imitation is mechanical, reflection organic.
The one is occasional, the other habitual. In the one case, man
comes to God and imitates Him; in the other, God comes to
man and imprints Himself upon Him. It is quite true that there
is an imitation of Christ which amounts to reflection. But Paul's
term includes all that the other holds, and is open to no mistake.

"Make Christ your most constant companion"—this is what it practically means for us. Be more under His influence than under any other influence. Ten minutes spent in his society every day, aye, two minutes if it be face to face, and heart to heart, will make the whole day different. Every character has an inward spring, let Christ be it. Every action has a keynote, let Christ set it. Yesterday you got a certain letter. You sat down and wrote a reply which almost scorched the paper. You picked the cruellest adjectives you knew and sent it forth, without a pang, to do its ruthless work. You did that because your life was set in the wrong key. You began the day with the mirror placed at the wrong angle. Tomorrow, at daybreak, turn it towards Him, and even to your enemy the fashion of your countenance wil be changed. Whatever you then do, one thing you will find you could not do—you could not write that letter. Your first impulse may be the same, your judgment may be unchanged, but if you try it the ink will dry on your pen, and you will rise from your desk an unavenged, but a greater and more Christian, man. Throughout the whole day your actions, down to the last detail, will do homage to that early vision. Yesterday, you thought mostly about yourself. Today the poor will meet you, and you will feed them. The helpless, the tempted, the sad, will throng about you, and each you will befriend. Where were all these people yesterday? Where they are today, but you did not see them. It is in reflected light that the poor are seen. But your soul today is not at the ordinary angle. "Things which are not seen" are visible. For a few short hours you live the Eternal Life. The eternal life, the life of faith, is simply the life of the higher vision. Faith is an attitude—a mirror set at the right angle.

When tomorrow is over, and in the evening you review it, you will wonder how you did it. You will not be conscious that you strove for anything, or imitated anything, or crucified anything. You will be conscious of Christ; that he was with you, that without compulsion you were yet compelled, that without force, or noise, or proclamation, the revolution was accomplished. You do not congratulate yourself as one who has done a mighty deed, or achieved a personal success, or stored up a fund of "Christian experience" to ensure the same result again. What you are conscious of is "the glory of the Lord"

And what the world is conscious of, if the result be a true one, is also "the glory of the Lord." In looking at a mirror one does not see the mirror, or think of it, but only of what it reflects. For a mirror never calls attention to itself—except when there are flaws in it.

That this is a real experience and not a vision, that this life is possible to men, is being lived by men today, is simple biographical fact. From a thousand witnesses I cannot forbear to summon one. The following are the words of one of the highest intellects this age has known, a man who shared the burdens of his country as few have done, and who, not in the shadows of old age, but in the high noon of his success, gave this confession —I quote it with only a few abridgments—to the world:

"I want to speak tonight only a little, but that little I desire to speak of the sacred name of Christ, who is my life, my inspiration, my hope, and my surety. I cannot help stopping and looking back upon the past. And I wish, as if I had never done it before, to bear witness, not only that it is by the grace of God, but that it is by the grace of God, as manifested in Christ Jesus, that I am what I am. I recognize the sublimity and grandeur of the revelation of God in His eternal fatherhood as one that made the heavens, that founded the earth, and that regards all the tribes of the earth, comprehending them in one universal merch; but it is the God that is manifested in Jesus Christ, revealed by His life, made known by the inflections of His feelings, by His discourse, and by His deeds—it is that God that I desire to confess tonight, and of whom I desire to say, 'By the love of God in Christ Jesus I am what I am.'

"If you ask me precisely what I mean by that, I say, frankly, that more than any recognized influence of my father or my mother upon me; more than the social influence of all the members of my father's household, more, so far as I can trace it, or so far as I am made aware of it, than all the social influences of every kind, Christ has had the formation of my mind and my disposition. My hidden ideals of what is beautiful I have drawn from Christ. My thoughts of what is manly, and noble, and pure, have almost all of them arisen from the Lord Jesus Christ. Many men have educated themselves by reading Plutarch's Lives of the Ancient Worthies, and setting before themselves one and another of these that in different ages have achieved celebrity; and they have recognized the great power of these men on themselves. Now I do not perceive that poet, or philosopher, or reformer, or general, or any other great man, ever has dwelt in my imagination and in my thought as the simple Jesus has. For more than twenty-five years I instinctively have gone to Christ to draw a measure and a rule for everything. Whenever there has been a necessity for it, I have sought—and at last almost spontaneously—to throw myself into the companionship of Christ; and early, by my imagination, I could see Him standing and looking quietly and lovingly upon me. There seemed almost to drop from His face an influence upon me that suggested what was the right thing in the controlling of passion, in the subduing of pride, in the overcoming of selfishness; and it is from Christ, manifested to my inward eye, that I have consciously derived more ideals, more models, more influences, than any other human character whatever.

"That is not all. I feel conscious that I have derived from the Lord Jesus Christ every thought that makes heaven a reality to me, and every thought that paves the road that lies between me and heaven. All my conceptions of the progress of grace in the soul; all the steps by which divine life is evolved; all the ideals that overhand the blessed sphere which awaits us beyond this world—these are derived from the Saviour. The life that I now live in the flesh I live by the faith of the Son of God.

"That is not all. Much as my future includes all these elements which go to make the blessed fabric of earthly life, yet, after all, what the summer is compared with all its earthly products—flowers, and leaves, and grass—that is Christ compared with all the products of Christ in my mind and in my soul. All the flowers and leaves of sympathy; all the twining joys that come from my heart as a Christian—these I take and hold in the future, but they are to me what the flowers and leaves of summer are compared with the sun that makes the summer. Christ is the Alpha and Omega, the beginning and the end of my better life.

"When I read the Bible, I gather a great deal from the Old Testament, and from the Pauline portions of the New Testament; but after all, I am conscious that the fruit of the Bible is Christ. That is what I read it for, and that is what I find that is worth reading. I have had a hunger to be loved of Christ. You all know, in some relations, what it is to be hungry for love. Your heart seems unsatisfied till you can draw something more toward you from those that are dearest to you. There have been times when I have had an unspeakable heart-hunger for Christ's love. My sense of sin is never strong when I think of the law; my sense of sin is strong when I think of love—if there is any difference between law and love. It is when drawing near the Lord Jesus Christ, and longing to be loved, that I have the most vivid sense of unsymmetry, of imperfection, of absolute unworthiness, and of my sinfulness. Character and conduct are never so vividly set before me as when in silence I bend in the presence of Christ, revealed not in wrath, but in love to me. I never so much long to be lovely, that I may be loved, as when I have this revelation of Christ before my mind.

"In looking back upon my experience, that part of my life which stands out, and which I remember most vividly, is just that part that has had some conscious association with Christ. All the rest is pale, and thin, and lies like clouds on the horizon. Doctrines, systems, measures, methods—what may be called the necessary mechanical and external part of worship; the part which the senses would recognize—this seems to have withered and fallen off like leaves of last summer; but that part which has taken hold of Christ abides."

Can anyone hear this life-music, with its throbbing refrain of Christ, and remain unmoved by envy or desire? Yet, till we have lived like this we have never lived at all.

THE FIRST EXPERIMENT

Then you reduce religion to a common Friendship? A common Friendship—who talks of a *common* Friendship? There is no such thing in the world. On earth no word is more sublime. Friendship is the nearest thing we know to what religion is. God is love. And to make religion akin to Friendship is simply to give it the highest expression conceivable by man. But if by demuring to "a common friendship" is meant a protest against the greatest and the holiest in religion being spoken of in intelligible terms, then I am afraid the objection is all too real. Men always look for a mystery when one talks of sanctification; some mystery apart from that which must ever be mysterious wherever Spirit works. It is thought some peculiar secret lies behind it, some occult experience which only the initiated know. Thousands of persons go to church every Sunday hoping to solve this mystery. At meetings, at conferences, many a time they have reached what they thought was the very brink of it, but somehow no further revelation came. Poring over religious books, how often were they not within a paragraph of it; the next page, the next sentence, would discover all, and they would be borne on a flowing tide forever. But nothing happened. The next sentence and the next page were read, and still it eluded them; and though the promise of its coming kept faithfully up to the end, the last chapter found them still pursuing. Why did nothing happen? Because there was nothing to happen—nothing of the kind they were looking for. Why did it elude them? Because there was no "it". When shall we learn that the pursuit of holiness is simply the pursuit of Christ? When shall we substitute for the "it" of a fictitious aspiration, the approach to a Living Friend? Sanctity is in character and not in moods; Divinity in our own plain calm humanity, and in no mystic rapture of the soul.

And yet there are others who, for exactly a contrary reason, will find scant satisfaction here. Their complaint is not that a religion expressed in terms of Friendship is too homely, but that it is still too mystical. To "abide" in Christ, to "make Christ our most constant companion", is to them the purest mysticism. They want something absolutely tangible and absolutely direct. These are not the poetical souls who seek a sign, a mysticism in excess; but the prosaic natures whose want is mathematical definition in details. Yet it is perhaps not possible to reduce this problem to much more rigid elements. The beauty of Friendship is its infinity. One can never evacuate life of mysticism. Home is full of it, love is full of it, religion is full or it. Why stumble at that in the relation of man to Christ which is natural in the relation of man to man?

If anyone cannot conceive or realize a mystical relation with Christ, perhaps all that can be done is to help him to step on to it by still plainer analogies from common life. How do I know Shakespeare or Dante? By communing with their words and thoughts. Many men know Dante better than their own fathers. He influences them more. As a spiritual presence he is more near to them, as a spiritual force more real. Is there any reason why a greater than Shakespeare or Dante, who also walked this earth, who left great words behind Him, who has greater works everywhere in the world now, should not also instruct, inspire, and mould the characters of men? I do not limit Christ's influence to this. It is this, and it is more. But Christ, so far from resenting or discouraging this relation of Friendship, Himself proposed it. "Abide in Me" was almost His last word to the world. And He partly met the difficulty of those who feel its intangibleness by adding the practical clause, "If ye abide in Me *and My words abide in you.*"

Begin with His words. Words can scarcely ever be long impersonal. Christ Himself was a Word, a word made Flesh. Make His words flesh; do them, live them, and you must live Christ. *"He that keepeth My commandments,* he it is that loveth Me." Obey Him and you must love Him. *Cultivate* His friendship. Live after Christ, in His Spirit, as in His Presence, and it is difficult to think what more you can do. Take this at least as a first lesson, as introduction. If you cannot at once and always feel the play of His life upon yours, watch for it also indirectly. "The whole earth is full of the character of the Lord." Christ is the Light of the world, and much of His Light is reflected from things in the world—even from clouds. Sunlight is stored in every leaf, from leaf through coal, and it comforts us thence when days are dark and we cannot see the sun. Christ shines through men, through books, through history, through nature, music, art. Look for Him there. "Every day one should either look at a beautiful picture, or hear beautiful music, or read a beautiful poem." The real danger of mysticism is not making it broad enough.

Do not think that nothing is happening because you do not see yourself grow, or hear the whirr of the machinery. All great things grow noiselessly. You can see a mushroom grow, but never a child . . . Paul knew that, and put it, only in more beautiful words, into the heart of his formula. He said for the comforting of all slowly perfecting souls that they grew "from character to character." "The inward man," he says elsewhere, "is renewed from day to day." All thorough work is slow; all true development by minute, slight, and insensible metamorphoses. The higher the structure, moreover, the slower the progress. As the biologist runs his eye over the long Ascent of Life he sees the lowest forms of animals develop in an hour; the next above these reach maturity in a day; those higher still take weeks or months to perfect but the few at the top demand the long experiment of years. If a child and an ape are born on the same day, the last will be in full possession of its faculties and doing the active work of life before the child has left the cradle. Life is the cradle of eternity. As the man is to the animal in the slowness of his growth, so is the spiritual man to the natural man. Foundations which have to bear the weight of an eternal life must be surely laid. Character is to wear forever; who will wonder or grudge that it cannot be developed in a day?

To await the growing of a soul, nevertheless, is an almost Divine act of faith. How pardonable, surely, the impatience of deformity with itself, of a consciously despicable character standing before Christ, wondering, yearning, hungering to be like that? Yet must one trust the process fearlessly, and without misgiving. "The Lord the Spirit" will do His part. The tempting expedient is, in haste for abrupt or visible progress, to try some method less spiritual, or to defeat the end by watching for effects instead of keeping the eye on the Cause. A photograph prints from the negative only while exposed to the sun. While the artist is looking to see how it is getting on he simply stops the getting on. Whatever of wise supervision the soul may need, it is certain it can never be over-exposed, or that, being exposed, anything else in the world can improve the result or quicken it. The creation of a new heart, the renewing of a right spirit, is an omnipotent work of God. Leave it to the Creator. "He which hath begun a good work in you will perfect it unto that day."

No man, nevertheless, who feels the worth and solemnity of what is at stake will be careless as to his progress. To become like Christ is the only thing in the world worth caring for, the thing before which every ambition of man is folly, and all lower achievement vain. Those only who make this quest the supreme desire and passion of their lives can ever begin to hope to reach it. If, therefore, it has seemed up to this point as if all depended on passivity, let me now assert, with conviction more intense, that all depends on activity. A religion of effortless adoration may be a religion for an angel, but never for a man. Not in the contemplative, but in the active, lies true hope; not in rapture, but in reality, lies true life; not in the realm of ideals, but among tangible things, is man's sanctification wrought. Resolution, effort, pain, self-crucifixion, agony—all the things already dismissed as futile in themselves must now be restored to office, and a tenfold responsibility laid upon them. For what is their office? Nothing less than to move the vast inertia of the soul, and place it, and keep it where the spiritual forces will act upon it. It is to rally the forces of the will, and keep the surface of the mirror bright and ever in position. It is to uncover the face which is to look at Christ, and draw down the veil when unhallowed sights are near. You have, perhaps, gone with an astronomer to watch him photograph the spectrum of a star. As you entered the dark vault of the observatory you saw him begin by lighting a candle. To see the star with? No; but to see to adjust the instrument to see the star with. It was the star that was going to take the photograph; it was, also, the astonomer. For a long time he worked in the dimness, screwing tubes and polishing lenses and adjusting reflectors, and only after much labor the finely focussed instrument was brought to bear. Then he blew out the light, and left the star to do its work upon the plate alone. The day's task for the Christian is to bring his instrument to bear. Having done that he may blow out his candle. All the evidences of Christianity which have brought him there, all aids to Faith, all acts of worship, all the leverages of the Church, all Prayer and Meditation, all girding of the Will—these lesser processes, these candle-light activities for that supreme hour, may be set aside. But, remember, it is but for an hour. The wise man will be he who quickest lights his candle; the wisest he who never lets it out. Tomorrow, the next moment, he, a poor, darkened, blurred soul, may need it again to focus the Image better, to take a mote off the lens, to clear the mirror from a breath with which the world has dulled it.

How Can I Be Filled With the Holy Spirit?

No readjustment is ever required on behalf of the Star. That is one great fixed point in this shifting universe. But *the world moves*. And each day, each hour, demands a further motion and readjustment for the soul. A telescope in an observatory follows a star by clockwork, but the clockwork of the soul is called *the Will*. Hence, while the soul in passivity reflects the Image of the Lord, the Will in intense activity holds the mirror in position lest the drifting motion of the world bear it beyond the line of vision. To "follow Christ" is largely to keep the soul in such position as will allow for the motion of the earth. And this calculated counteracting of the movements of the world, this holding of the mirror exactly opposite to the Mirrored, this steading of the faculties unerringly through cloud and earthquake, fire and sword, is the stupendous co-operating labor of the Will. It is all man's work. It is all Christ's work. In practice it is both; in theory it is both. But the wise man will say in practice, "It depends upon myself."

In the Galerie des Beaux Arts in Paris there stands a famous statue. It was the last work of a great genius, who, like many a genius, was very poor and lived in a garret, which served as a studio and sleeping-room alike. When the statue was all but finished, one midnight a sudden frost fell upon Paris. The sculptor lay awake in the fireless room and thought of the still moist clay, thought how the water would freeze in the pores and destroy in an hour the dream of his life. So the old man rose from his couch and heaped the bed clothes reverently round his work. In the morning when the neighbors entered the room the sculptor was dead. But the statue lived.

The Image of Christ that is forming within us—that is life's one charge. Let every project stand aside for that. "Till Christ be formed," no man's work is finished, no religion crowned, no life has fulfilled its end. Is the infinite task begun? When, how, are we to be different? Time cannot change men. Death cannot change men. Christ can. Wherefore *put on* Christ.

Examination over Lesson Six

1. How do we relate to the subject of being filled with the Holy Spirit? Is it optional? imperative? relative? — Please discuss.
2. In understanding II Cor. 3:18 explain the following terms: "unveiled face"—"mirror"—"the glory of the Lord"—"the

same image"—"from glory to glory"—"as from the Lord the Spirit."

3. Give in your own words the meaning of Romans 13:14.
4. Discuss three veils *not* discussed in this lesson that we must remove before we can behold His glory.
5. Suggest a definite program in which we can come to know our Lord in the personal powerful way we want to.
6. What part of Drummond's *Formula Of Sanctification* appealed to you most? Tell why.

Lesson Seven
HOW CAN I HAVE THE FRUIT OF THE SPIRIT?

There surely can be no question in your mind as to how to go about developing the wonderful virtues of the Holy Spirit within your life. Jesus our Lord is and was the personification of each of these qualities. Our Lord was the incarnation of:

love — joy — peace — longsuffering — kindness — goodness — faithfulness — meekness — self-control.

Do we understand the love of our Lord in such a way as to make it a powerful living force in our heart? There are many, many books written to show how Jesus loved—and I have read some of them. This is not enough—His love *must* be our love. *The Holy Spirit must give life to the letter within us!* There is so much to learn of His love—His love for man—His love for God. The most we can do in these lessons (and perhaps the best) is to suggest the procedure by which a fullness or maturity of love can be developed by every sincere student.

This material will almost take the form of a soliloquy for the very good reason—I need so desperately to develop these virtues in my own personality. If this seems to be very personal in places it is because it is!

Do you want the Holy Spirit to produce *His love* in your character? (We are sure you do or you would not have read this far in our study.) Let's look at the love of Jesus and ask the Holy Spirit to make Him real within us. We shall arrange this in a nine week study—(one week for each of the blessed virtues). There will be a *daily readings* and *questions,* then a comment for the week to close each study. We will print out certain references—others we will offer as comparative texts—in this way we can produce a rather complete study on each subject.

THE FRUIT OF THE SPIRIT IS *LOVE*

We can easily say "the result of the indwelling Christ is love". *First Day.*

Luke 6:27, 28: "But I say unto you which hear, Love your enemies, do good to them which hate you, Bless them that curse you, and pray for them which despitefully use you."

Luke 6:32-38: "For if ye love them which love you, what

45

thank have ye? for sinners also love those that love them. And if ye do good to them which do good to you, what thank have ye? for sinners also do even the same. And if ye lend to them of whom ye hope to receive, what thank have ye? for sinners also lend to sinners, to receive as much again. But love ye your enemies, and do good, and lend, hoping for nothing again; and your reward shall be great, and ye shall be the children of the Highest: for he is kind unto the unthankful and to the evil. Be ye therefore merciful, as your Father also is merciful. Judge not, and ye shall not be judged: condemn not, and ye shall not be condemned: forgive, and ye shall be forgiven: Give, and it shall be given unto you; good measure, pressed down, and shaken together, and running over, shall men give into your bosom. For with the same measure that ye mete withal it shall be measured to you again."

Please notice at the very outset that not everyone who has ears can hear! There are spiritually deaf folk among us.— *The words of Jesus are only spoken to those who hear.* Is there some hesitancy in my heart to open up my inner ear to let the words of Jesus fall upon my conscience?

Pray this prayer with me: "Holy Spirit of God—let me be tenderly sensitive—eagerly responsive to the words of my Lord. Let them divide the thoughts and intents of my heart into the areas where *He* wants them to be."

Someone said "love for your enemies" is an *"overflowing good-will* toward unfriendly people." This should be—and *can be* our attitude toward all who are unfriendly to us. With such an attitude we can act with sincerity in doing good to and for such persons. Jesus seems to be suggesting that we kill our enemies with kindness. He supplies the ammunition—here it is: (1) over-flowing good will; (2) do them good—(do some good thing for them); (3) bless them—i.e. ask God's grace and direction in their lives—(do this with no thought of revenge but only of good-will); (4) offer definite personal prayer for those who despitefully use you. Another one has well said: "Read this passage over, using it as a window to look into Jesus' own heart." He actually had such an attitude toward His enemies! It is *not* impossible. Jesus lived "in the likeness of (our) sinful flesh" and practiced what He here taught.

How Can I Have the Fruit of the Spirit?

We must go much further than those about us who do not love Jesus. How much further do we go? Consider: (1) love those who do not love you; (2) do good to those who will not return the favor; (3) lend to those who will not return the loan; (4) be kind and merciful to the unthankful and evil; (5) do not condemn or judge those who apparently need it; (6) release what you would like to keep—but which if released would do another more good than it would if kept for yourself. (This can refer to money—any possession—or to your time— your words); (7) give—the way to receive is to give. When will we in truth—in fact—not in theory—believe this?

In the above seven areas Jesus expressed His love. Please read them and relate them to your life. Remember we have the promised help of the Holy Spirit (Ephesians 3:16) to develop this virtue in our personalities. Once again—to love like Jesus loved means: (1) love those who do not love you. This could refer to many people who do not even know you—as well as to those who are unfriendly. Jesus had an "overflowing good-will toward unfriendly people". Pray with me: "Holy Spirit of God —help me to adopt this attitude!" (2) to love as Jesus loved means to do good to those who will not return the favor. May I be more than idealistic about this? What good can I do for someone who cannot return the favor? There are folk in rest homes—hopsitals—jails—to whom such love could be expressed. Perhaps I even have relatives to whom such love could be given. Pray with me: "Lord—Holy Spirit—help me to *do*—not *dream* about this." (3) to love as Jesus loved means—to lend to those who will not return the loan. Please notice there is a difference in a gift and a loan. Can I not approximate a circumstance in the life of our Lord in which such an expression of His love was seen—and then go and do likewise? What about the healing power of Jesus? Wasn't this a loan of God to sick mankind? Can I not offer to loan my time or talents in some "sick" area of life? Do it—like our Lord did—because He did—because He in you prompts you to! (4) to love as Jesus did means to be kind and merciful to the unthankful and evil. What a shock some people would get if this were true in our life! Who are the unthankful and evil in your neighborhood? Do you have any on the job where you work? Are there any on the church board?

(Surely not!) Could we recognize kindness if we saw it? Most of us could. "Mercy" means a willingness to forgive and help in an area where it is not deserved. (5) to love as Jesus did means not to condemn or judge those who apparently need it. This is not a reference to condoning sin or indulging wickedness. There are so very many areas in our lives where we condemn (criticize—gripe—complain). There are so many people we can (and do) write off as no good—stupid—ignorant—or in some other way beneath us. To such circumstances and persons, dear Lord, help me to give love! (6) to love as Jesus did (and does) means to release what I would like to keep. This presupposes that good could come from the release. "He who was rich became poor—that we through His poverty might become rich." "He counted not the being an equal to God something to hold—*but to release.*" How rich we have become because He did. Do I now have any money I could (or would) release with the bare—remote possibility it would do more good than if kept? What about my time? my possessions—which one of them will I release to save the lost world? (7) to love as Jesus did (and does) is to give. Love is not a sentimental feeling, but a very tangible expression seen in actions and gifts. Pray with me: "Wonderful Lord—powerful Holy Spirit—chastise me—direct my decisions—open doors that I may be filled with the love of our Lord—not in word but in deed and in truth."
Second Day.

Matthew 18:21-30. "Then came Peter to him, and said, Lord, how oft shall my brother sin against me, and I forgive him? till seven times? Jesus saith unto him, I say not unto thee, Until seven times: but, Until seventy times seven. Therefore is the kingdom of heaven likened unto a certain king, which would take account of his servants. And when he had begun to reckon, one was brought unto him, which owed him ten thousand talents. But forasmuch as he had not to pay, his Lord commanded him to be sold, and his wife, and children, and all that he had, and payment to be made. The servant therefore fell down, and worshipped him, saying, Lord, have patience with me, and I will pay thee all. Then the lord of that servant was moved with compassion, and loosed him and forgave him the debt. But the same servant went out, and found one of his fellow-servants, which owed him an hundred pence: and he laid hands on him and took him by the throat, saying, Pay me that thou owest. And his fellow-servant fell down at his feet, and besought him, saying, Have patience with me, and I will pay thee all. And he would not: but went and cast him into prison, till he should pay the debt."

Here is the real test of love. How do we react—not how do we act—but how do we respond when acted upon? Are we willing to give when sinned against? Must we have a worthy recipient for our gift before we are willing to give? What happens to that feeling of "overflowing good will" when someone expresses selfishness or ill-will toward us? The nature or quality of our love is now made known. It is Christ-like—God-like or only as the publicans who "love those who love them"? Jesus says that holding a grudge is a sin. Do we believe this?

I think we should congratulate Peter—if he meant that he was willing to forgive from the heart seven times. He is much better than many of us. How beyond and above human ability are the words of our Lord—"until seventy times seven". The secret of acquiring such love is found in the parable of the unjust steward. (Read it again.) Please notice some of the obvious applications of our Lord's words to our conscience: (1) This is a parable about "the kingdom of heaven". We understand the kingdom of heaven to be the Church of our Lord—so this is a parable of our contemporary situation. We had best give careful attention to His words for us! (2) "The king"—"The reckoning"—"The servant"—"The ten thousand talents" (at least one million dollars). These are all transparent in meaning. The king is our God. The reckoning is the judgment. We are the servants. The million or more dollars is what we owe God. In other words, because of our sins we are bankrupt before God. (3) How much has God loved us in forgiving us? What is the quality of that love? (4) We all have "fellow-servants" who owe us something because they have sinned against us. (5) We will go to hell if we do not forgive as we have been forgiven.

Please notice that we are being forgiven by God, our King, every day. This is a continuing love graciously given to us by God.

The secret of forgiving love is contained in two truths: (1)

The deep, heartfelt appreciation we constantly hold for our forgiveness; (2) A realization of what it would mean to again be "delivered to the tormentors". We do not forgive one another from the heart because we do not know what it means to be forgiven by God. What did it cost God to forgive us? What did it cost our Lord? Can we condemn in another what we find in ourselves? "Herein is love, not that we loved God, but that He loved us, and sent his Son to be the propitiation (covering) for our sins. *Beloved, if God so loved us, we ought also to love one another,* (I John 4:10, 11).

Add to this the truth that if we do not forgive one another freely—continually—from the heart we will not be forgiven. Jesus made the provision—"forgive us our sins (trespasses) *as we also forgive those who sin (or trespass) against us.* (Matthew 6:12-15). (Cf. Mark 11:25)
Third Day.

Matthew 5:21-24. "Ye have heard that it was said by them of old time, Thou shalt not kill; and whosoever shall kill shall be in danger of the judgment: But I say unto you, That whosoever is angry with his brother without a cause shall be in danger of the judgment: and whosoever shall say to his brother, Raca, shall be in danger of the council: but whosoever shall say, Thou fool, shall be in danger of hell fire. Therefore if thou bring thy gift to the altar, and there rememberest that thy brother hath ought against thee; Leave there thy gift before the altar, and go thy way; first be reconciled to thy brother, and then come and offer thy gift."

Love as Jesus loved? Are we willing? ". . . out of the abundance of the heart the mouth speaketh". Words are the barometer of the heart. "By thy words thou art justified and by thy words art thou condemned". Let us love in words as well as deeds. How lightly we speak ill of our brother. What little matters call from us the condemnation of one another! Of what value is any religious act or form if we have "ought against our brother" or we remember he feels ill toward us?

Here are a few thoughtful questions on these verses:
(1) What "judgment" does Jesus have in mind as in vs. 22?
(2) Just what type of anger is involved in vs. 22? Are we excused for some type of anger with our brother? (Dis-

cuss, but be careful that we do not rationalize the circumstances so as to make void the words of our Lord.)

(3) Why is our Lord so stringent with the subject of anger (no surface answer here—please—look into your own heart *before* you answer.)

(4) Did Jesus really mean what He said about speaking contemptuously about our brothers? Would such expressions as "knot head", "stupid", "sap", "ignoramus" take the place of "Raca"? Are we to understand we cannot use these words when speaking contemptuously of our brothers? What words can we use?

(5) Have you ever been tempted to damn someone to hell because of his actions or attitude toward you? (Please say "yes" because we would hate to feel we were the only once who felt this way.) Jesus knew we would so react to some people and for this reason said what He did in vs. 22b. Please notice the progression in animosity as given in these verses:
   (1) Angry with your brother,
   (2) Contemptuous with your brother,
   (3) Condemning your brother.

(Please remember all men are brothers in the area of this need. Even if we do not remember or believe this we have enough members of the same church where we are a member to which this applies.)

Now notice the reversal of the order. We are about to drop the one dollar bill into the collection plate. We suddenly are reminded by someone or something of the animosity we hold in our heart toward one of our brothers—or sisters. We might even speak contemptuously about them under our breath—or at least form such words in our minds. If such is the case— *we have not loved—we do not love as Jesus loved.* Obviously Jesus never felt this way or spoke in such a manner about anyone. Is Christ in your heart? Pray this prayer with me: "Holy Spirit of God—by Thy Divine fire, burn out the dross in my nature. I do want to love as our Lord did. Enable me where I am not able of myself to love those who are so very unlovely. Deliver me from the bondage of ill-will—and grudge-holding. If God or Jesus held a grudge against me I would be lost indeed."

51

Fourth Day.

I Peter 2:21-24: "For even hereunto were ye called: because Christ also suffered for us, leaving us an example, that ye should follow his steps: Who did no sin, neither was guile found in his mouth: Who, when he was reviled, reviled not again; when he suffered, he threatened not; but committed himself to him that judgeth righteously: Who his own self bare our sins in his own body on the tree, that we being dead to sins, should live unto righteousness: by whose stripes ye were healed."

Please notice the context of verse 21. Read from verse 18. To what does "hereunto" refer? Hereunto what? Read John 15:20. In what particular sense are the sufferings of Christ an example for us? Specify two or three qualities of love we can follow in the sufferings of Jesus. Are we to understand the footprints of Jesus are close enough together (figuratively speaking) for us to step in them? In other words—is not the example of our Lord too exalted for us? If it isn't, why do we not follow it? Isn't this an obvious indication of the essential value of the power of the Holy Spirit? Read Romans 7:24, 25—8:1 and then Ephesians 3:16. How does "guile" relate to love? If you do not know the author can say from observation and sad experience that there is much guile that passes off for love. It is much easier to pretend or exaggerate, or ignore than it is to face up squarely to our own need. To love like our Lord is expressed when we live like our Lord. When we find ourselves in circumstances like His—when men begin to reproach and heap abuse on us and we do not return abuse for abuse. When someone unjustly calls you a name what do you say? When you are unfairly accused what do you do? If we love like our Lord we commit them and ourselves to the righteous judge. We refuse to take judgment and condemnation into our own hands.

Fifth Day.

Ephesians 4:25-32: "Wherefore putting away lying, speak every man truth with his neighbor: for we are members one of another. Be ye angry, and sin not: let not the sun go down upon your wrath: Neither give place to the devil. Let him that stole steal no more: but rather let him labour, working with his hands the thing which is good, that he may have to give to him that needeth. Let no corrupt communication proceed out of your mouth, but that which is good to the use of edifying, that it may minister grace unto the hearers. And grieve not the Holy Spirit of God, whereby ye are sealed unto the day of redemption. Let all bitterness, and wrath, and anger, and clamour, and evil speaking, be put away from you, with all malice: And be ye kind one to another, tenderhearted, forgiving one another, even as God for Christ's sake hath forgiven you."

Please notice the connective purpose of "Wherefore". On what ground or basis does Paul ask us to demonstrate all of these glorious virtues? How could Paul dare to use the past tense in speaking of "falsehood"? Read Zechariah 8:16 and Colossians 3:9 for good comparative references. (Zech. 8:16 is more than a comparative reference.) Why not say "we are all members of one body"? In what sense are we "members one of another"? Please, please make personal application of the principle here stated. How does *love* become the dominant need in the attempt to always tell the truth? Someone has suggested that the expression "Be angry" could be translated "tremble—or to stand in awe". It thus becomes a means of escaping sin. If we could live can make irritation temporary? You know the answer. Here is constantly aware of God we would not only "persuade men" (II Cor. 5:11) but would experience the effects of the most powerful antidote prescribed by God to prevent disobedience. But suppose we do become angry with our brother (hardly a supposition). Is it always necessary to let this anger lead to sin? Is not God angry with sin—not with the sinner? Wasn't our blessed Lord full of indignation at all forms of sin? Are we not commanded to "abhor that which is evil," (Rom. 12:9)? *Only love* can purify our anger. Only love can give us the unselfish insight past our neighbor's actions and words to his real need before God. To Jesus, actions of hatred and opposition were but signals of need—these were flags of distress—because He thought of His neighbors in this light He felt no personal animosity toward them. The two phrases in verse 26 can be thought of as separate entities—i.e. if you are angry with your neighbor, do not sustain it past the setting of the sun. What ingredient in our character will keep us from holding a grudge? What power in the practical day-by-day application of love. Occasion or scope is given to Satan through anger. Under the intoxicating influence of irritation we say and do many things that would not be done apart from this power of evil to distort our judgment. How much is love needed—it too is a strong intoxicant—from God. Under the impulse of love we say and do things we would never do without it. To acknowledge the need to "put away falsehood", "to not be selfishly angry", "to hold no grudge" is one thing. To have the power to carry into action such virtues is simply not in man apart from the enablement of the Holy Spirit through His love.

Let us not fail to remember there are various methods of stealing—but all stealing has its root in "the love of money". The answer of every problem of stealing is found in a transfer of the object of our affections—we can not love our God or our neighbor and practice any form of thievery. By love not only is the negative sin of stealing removed but the positive action of serving our neighbor is initiated. What will purify our hearts—our minds—our motives—so our speech will be pure? Oh my God, what power is there to enable me to cleanse my mouth? Whatever power there is—we need it!
The Sixth Day.

Mark 2:15-17: And it came to pass, that he was sitting at meat in his house, and many publicans and sinners sat down with Jesus and his disciples: for there were many, and they followed him. And the scribes of the Pharisees, when they saw that he was eating with the sinners and publicans, said unto his disciples, How is it that he eateth and drinketh with publicans and sinners? And when Jesus heard it, he saith unto them, They that are whole have no need of a physician, but they that are sick: I came not to call the righteous, but sinners.

Please attempt to identify present-day publicans and sinners. Please also notice the friendliness (and respect) existant with the sinners and our Lord. There was something attractive about Jesus—this was the reason they were with Him and He with them. That ethereal-elusive quality of concern must permeate our beings before sinners will see it or feel it. Love gives us an unselfish genuine interest in others. Here are a few questions to probe our conscience and make revelant what we have said:

(1) Isn't one of our biggest sins substituting going to church for going to sinners?

(2) When will we ever break out of our little circle of friends and *reach* with sincere personal interest (love) the publicans in our area of living?

(3) There are several types of monasteries—we need to climb over the wall and drop down into the midst of sinners— Jesus did! Let me list some of the protestant monasteries: (1) Bible College, (2) The local church, (3) Secular, Christian College, (4) Our own Christian family and friends, (5) Our denomination.

Jesus knew why He came into this world—He said, "I come not to call the righteous, but sinners." Why did I come? The presence or absence of real love will give the answer.
Seventh Day.

Luke 23:33, 34: And when they came unto the place which is called The Skull, there they crucified him, and the malefactors, one on the right hand and the other on the left. And Jesus said, Father, forgive them; for they know not what they do. And parting his garments among them, they cast lots.

We have not used all the references in the Gospel accounts expressing the love of our Lord. In the ones we have used we hope you have learned two truths; (1) How beautiful and powerful is love as personified in our Lord; (2) How unattainable such a virtue is without the aid of the Holy Spirit.

We look now for a few minutes at the last expression of His love—"and Jesus said, "Father forgive them; for they know not what they do." Is this not also true of everyone who sins against us? If anyone felt he was sinning against God would he not hesitate before he sinned? Is not all sin against God?—but we are but faintly aware of this—and so we sin not knowing what we do. This does not excuse anyone—we could know what we are doing if we wanted to—but this does insulate us from the frustration and animosity we sometimes (most of the time) feel toward those who hurt us. What is this insulation?—this cushion? It is the capacity to see the actions of men through the eyes of God—yea more—through the eyes of Jesus!

Please notice the decision to forgive was left up to the Father—it was against God that these men had sinned. For the Saviour's part they were forgiven—He held no ill-will toward them—the final decision was up to God—Jesus felt no hatred toward them — He committed them unto Him who judges righteously.

Pray with me (and for me): "Dear God, I have not yet been crucified—indeed I have not yet resisted unto blood striving against sin—but it takes so little to irritate me. Great God chastise me—purify by experience my motives. May I learn to love and forgive as did Thy Son."

Comment For The Week
LIKE CHRIST—In His love.
Andrew Murray

A new commandment I give unto you, That ye love one another; even as I have loved you, that ye also love one another.—John 13:34.

This is my commandment, That ye love one another, even as I have loved you.—John 15:12.

EVEN AS: We begin to understand somewhat of the blessedness of that little word. It is not the command of a law which only convinces of sin and impotence; it is a new command under a new covenant, that is established upon better promises. It is the command of Him who asks nothing that He has not provided, and now offers to bestow. It is the assurance that He expects nothing from us that He does not work in us: EVEN AS I have loved you, and every moment am pouring out that love upon you through the Holy Spirit, EVEN so do ye love one another. The measure, the strength, and the work of your love you will find in my love to you.

EVEN AS I have loved you: that word gives us the *measure* of the love wherewith we must love each other. True love knows no measure: it gives itself entirely. It may take into consideration the time and measure of showing it; but love itself entirely. It may take into consideration the time and measure of showing it; but love itself is ever whole and undivided. This is the greatest glory of divine love that we have, in the Father and Son, two persons, who in love remain One Being, each losing Himself in the other. This is the glory of the love of Jesus, who is the image of God, that He loves us even as the Father loves Him. And this is the glory of brotherly love, that it will know of no other law than to love even as God and Christ.

He who would be like Christ must unhesitatingly accept this as his rule of life. He knows how difficult, how impossible it often is thus to love brethren, in whom there is so much that is offensive or unamiable. Before going out to meet them in circumstances where his love may be tried, he goes in secret to the Lord, and with his eyes fixed on his own sin and unworthiness asks: How much owest thou thy Lord? He goes to the cross and seeks there to fathom the love wherewith the Lord has loved him. He lets the light of the immeasurable love of Him who is in heaven, his Head and his Brother, shine in upon his soul, until he learns to feel divine love has but one law: love seeks not its own, love gives itself wholly. And he lays himself on the altar before his Lord: even as Thou hast loved me, so will I love the brethren. In virtue of my union with Jesus, and in Jesus with them, there can be no question of anything less: I love them as Christ did. Oh, that Christians would close their ears to all the reasonings of their own hearts, and fix their eyes only on the law which He who loves them has promulgated in His own example: They would realize that there is nothing for them to do but this, —to accept His commands and to obey them.

Our love may recognize no other measure than His, because His love is *the strength* of ours. The love of Christ is no mere idea or sentiment; it is a real divine life-power. As long as the Christian does not understand this, it cannot exert its full power in him. But when his faith rises to realize that Christ's love is nothing less than the imparting of Himself and His love to the beloved, and he becomes rooted in this love as the source whence his life derives its sustenance, then he sees that his Lord simply asks that he should allow His love to flow through Him. He must live in a Christ-given strength: the love of Christ constrains him, and enables him to love as He did.

From this love of Christ the Christian also learns what *the work* of his love to the brethren must be. We have already had occasion to speak of many manifestations of love: its loving service, its self-denial, its meekness. Love is the root of all these. It teaches the disciple to look upon himself as really called upon to be, in his little circle, just like Jesus, the one who lives solely to love and help others. Paul prays for the Philippians: "That your love may abound more and more in knowledge, and in all judgment" (Phil. i.9). Love does not comprehend at once what the work is that it can do. The believer who prays that his love may abound in knowledge, and really takes Christ's example as his rule of life, will be taught what a great and glorious work there is for him to do. The Church of God, and every child of God, as well as the world, has an unspeakable need of love, of the manifestation of Christ's love. The Christian who really takes the Lord's word, "Love one another *even* as I have loved you," as a command that must be obeyed, carries about a power for blessing and life for all with whom he comes in contact. Love is the explanation of the whole wonderful life of Christ, and of the wonder of His death; divine love in God's children will still work its mighty wonders.

"Behold what manner of love!" "Behold how He loved!" These words are the superscription over the love of the Father and of the Son. They must yet become the key-words to the life of every Christian. They will be so where in living faith and true consecration the command of Christ to love, even as He loved, is accepted as the law of life. As early as the call of Abraham this principle was deposited as a living seed in God's kingdom, that what God is for us we must be for others. "I will bless thee," "and thou shalt be a blessing." If "I have loved you" is the highest manifestation of what God is for us, the "Even so love ye" must be the first and highest expression of what the child of God must be. In preaching, as in the life of the Church, it must be understood: *The love which loves like Christ is the sign of true discipleship.*

Beloved Christians, Christ Jesus longs for you in order to make you, amid those who surround you, a very fountain of love. The love of Heaven would fain take possession of you, in order that, in and through you, it may work its blessed work on earth. Yield to its rule. Offer yourself unreservedly to its indwelling. Honour it by the confident assurance that it can teach you to love as Jesus loved. As conformity to the Lord Jesus must be the chief mark of your Christian walk, so love must be the chief mark of that conformity. Be not disheartened if you do not attain it at once. Only keep fast hold of the command, "Love even as I have loved you." It takes time to grow into it. Take time in secret to gaze on that image of love. Take time in prayer and meditation to fan the desire for it into a burning flame. Take time to survey all around you, whoever they be, and whatever may happen, with this one thought, "I must love them." Take time to become conscious of your union with your Lord, that every fear as to the possibility of thus loving may be met with the word: "Have not I commanded you: Love as I have loved?" Christian, take time in loving communion with Jesus, your loving example, and you will joyfully fulfill this command, too, to love even as He did.

Lord Jesus, who hast loved me so wonderfully and now commandest me to love even as Thou, behold me at Thy feet. Joyfully would I accept Thy commands, and now go out in Thy strength to manifest Thy love to all.

In Thy strength, O my Lord, be therefore pleased to reveal Thy love to me. Shed abroad Thy love in my heart through Thy Holy Spirit. Let me live each moment in the experience that I am the beloved of God.

Lord, let me understand that I can love, not with my own, but with Thy love. Thou livest in me, Thy Spirit dwells and works in me; from Thee there streams into me the love with which I can love others. Thou dost only ask of me that I understand and accept Thy calling, and that I surrender myself to live as Thou didst. Thou wouldst that I look upon my old nature with its selfishness and unlovingness as crucified, and in faith prepare to do as Thou commandest.

Lord, I do it. In the strength of my Lord, I would live *to love even as Thou hast loved me*. Amen.

(LIKE CHRIST, ANDREW MURRAY, pp. 125-130)

THE FRUIT OF THE SPIRIT IS JOY
We believe the result of the indwelling Christ is joy!

First Day.

John 15:11; 16:22; 17:13; 11 These things have I spoken unto you, that my joy may be in you, and that your joy may be made full. 22 And ye therefore now have sorrow: but I will see you again, and your heart shall rejoice, and your joy no one taketh away from you. 13 But now I come to thee; and these things I speak in the world, that they may have my joy made full in themselves.

We have the priceless privilege of having the joy of Jesus in us. But do we know what made Jesus happy? Someone so very well said: "Consider the exhaustless sources of Jesus' joy: (1) His trust in His Father, (2) His boundless hope for the future, (3) His consciousness that He had found and was doing God's will for Him, (4) His sense of God's approval on His life, (5) His knowledge that He was doing a great and abiding service for men."

Whereas emotional response to any circumstance is not as important as the circumstance, or the reason for the circumstance, we yet believe Jesus was emotionally involved in these reasons for joy. He was full of enthusiastic good will. His outlook on life was one of "good cheer". What kind of emotional reaction do we get from the five areas of our Lord's happiness?:

(1) Are we full of joy in our confident trust in God?—is not our trust much more of a passive experience?—is there never a time for exuberance in our expression of trust?

(2) Are we always rejoicing in the hope of heaven? Are we confidently satisfied that Jesus has and does, and will "overcome the world"?

(3) Are the energies of our life extended in a spiritually profitable enterprise? "Only one life—and it will soon be past, Only what is done for Christ will last."—is what we are now doing profitable in the service of Christ?

(4) All of us fail from time to time (or even twice in a time) but as we look back over the past several years we can believe Christ approves of our choices.

(5) The deepest satisfactions are found in a great and abiding service for others—is that our investment of life? If we do not have these sources for joy then we can not have the fruit of the Spirit.

Second Day.

Matthew 5:3-12: Blessed are the poor in spirit: for theirs is the kingdom of heaven. Blessed are they that mourn: for they shall be comforted. Blessed are the meek: for they shall inherit the earth. Blessed are they that hunger and thirst after righteousness: for they shall be filled. Blessed are the merciful: for they shall obtain mercy. Blessed are the pure in heart: for they shall see God. Blessed are the peacemakers: for they shall be called sons of God. Blessed are they that have been persecuted for righteousness' sake: for theirs is the kingdom of heaven. Blessed are ye when men shall reproach you, and persecute you, and say all manner of evil against you falsely, for my sake. Rejoice, and be exceedingly glad: for great is your reward in heaven: for so persecuted they the prophets that were before you.

Perhaps we could call the Beatitudes "the conditions of happiness"—the word "blessed" has been translated by some as "happy"—it carries a deeper meaning than we usually associate with "happiness"—*"satisfied* or *"complete"* would be a better word. What are the conditions of satisfaction or completeness?— Give them a long look: (1) poor in spirit, (2) they that mourn, (3) meekness, (4) hunger and thirst after righteousness, (5) merciful, (6) pure in heart, (7) peacemaker, (8) persecuted for righteousness sake.

How completely removed is all selfishness and self-satisfaction on a material or animal level in the conditions of happiness indicated by our Saviour! The fruit or the result of the Spirit's indwelling is *joy*—but here is the fountain out of which this joy flows. Here is a picture of the joyful heart. "Lord, I believe, help Thou my unbelief."

Third Day.

Matthew 13:44; 25:21-23: 44 The kingdom of heaven is like unto a treasure hidden in the field; which a man found, and hid; and in his joy he goeth and selleth all that he hath, and buyeth that field. 21-23 His lord said unto him, Well done, good and faithful servant: thou hast been faithful over a few things, I well set thee over many things; enter thou into the joy of thy lord. And he also that received the two talents came and said, Lord, thou deliveredst unto me two talents: lo, I have gained other two talents. His lord said unto him, Well done, good and faithful servant: thou hast been faithful over a few things, I will set thee over many things; enter thou into the joy of thy lord.

What did Jesus mean in His use of the term "the kingdom of heaven"? He meant "the rule of God in the life of man"— this became a reality in the "called out ones" of whom Jesus spoke when He said "I will build my church," (Matt. 16:18). How could membership in Christ's church be compared to the discovery of a buried treasure? This is ridiculous! Church membership is not as exciting as the discovery of buried treasure— Church membership is not as valuable as buried treasure (that is, on a cash basis). Dig a little deeper—this is why Jesus said it was "buried"—"hidden". If the reality of the forgiveness of sins and acceptance with God our Father would ever break through our flesh-bound consciousness in all its reality we would be like the man in the parable—*full of joy!*

Read again Matthew 25:21-23 and then read this little gem of literature: "When we give up an immediate pleasure for character's sake, we are impressed with how much we have sacrificed. Jesus was impressed with how much a man had gained. Consider what you have gained by any sacrifice you ever made for Character; (1) the approval of God through conscience, (2) the satisfaction of overcomnig your moral enemy (Satan), (3) the greater power to conquer the next time, (4) the approbation of those who care most for you, (5) you have increased your power of usefulness to others. How much more have you gained than you sacrificed? Ought not all such sacrifice to be made with joy? Nobody ever found any real, solid, and permanent satisfaction in doing wrong."

Fourth Day.

Luke 15:3-10: And he spake unto them this parable, saying, What man of you, having a hundred sheep, and having lost one of them, doth not leave the ninety and nine in the wilderness, and go after that which is lost, until he find it? And when he hath found it, he layeth it on his shoulders, rejoicing. And when he cometh home, he calleth together his friends and his neighbors, saying unto them, Rejoice with me, for I have found my sheep which was lost. I say unto you, that even so there shall be joy in heaven over one sinner that repenteth, more than over ninety and nine righteous persons, who need no repentance. Or what woman having ten pieces of silver, if she lose one piece, doth not light a lamp, and sweep the house, and seek diligently until she find it? And when she hath found it, she calleth together her friends and neighbors, saying, Rejoice with me, for I have found the piece which I had lost. Even so, I say unto you, there is joy in the presence of the angels of God over one sinner that repenteth.

What word of joy and rejoicing will we give to our neighbors and friends? Can we honestly say to them *"Rejoice* with me for I have found my sheep which was lost"? We constantly pray "Thy will be done on earth *as it is* in heaven"—Jesus said the angels are happy over the repentance of sinners—do we really want our prayer answered—? Are we personally—emotionally involved in seeking and saving lost sheep? Where is the joy of the soul winner? The fruit of the Holy Spirit (whose mission is to woo lost sinners) is *joy!* Joy is the fruit of a heart condition.

There is no happiness comparable to that of the one who has gone forth weeping; bearing precious seed for sowing—and now comes bringing his sheaves with him into the eternal garner. There are reasons for the depth of this joy; it relates to eternity —not time—it relates to people—eternal spirits—not earth-bound things—"A man's life (joy) does not consist in the abundance of *things* he possesses." So said our Lord whose true joy was in seeking and saving the lost.

Fifth Day.

Matthew 6:28,29: And why are ye anxious concerning raiment? Consider the lilies of the field, how they grow; they toil not, neither do they spin: yet I say unto you, that even Solomon in all his glory was not arrayed like one of these.

Here is the biggest enemy to joy—*anxiety*—this but indicates the source of our enjoyment—if our joy was obtained from the five sources of Jesus' joy (as indicated earlier) we would not be anxious.

"But"—I can hear someone say—"I must be responsible— every Christian must share material and sometimes rather earthly responsibilities—we can not be obligated for payments and material possessions without a certain amount of anxiety." Let's analyze this carefully: Are we to assume that responsibility equals anxiety?—did anyone ever have greater responsibilities (and deadlines) than our Lord? He was not anxious. There is joy in sharing the responsibilities of heaven—when our highest happiness is in our trust in God—in our consciousness that we are doing His will there will be no anxiety. Jesus associated anxiety with raiment—food and possessions—when our life (time-energy-talent-money-thought) is taken up with care and use of "things"—we inevitably become worried and "cumbered about". Choose the area of the investment of your life—"Seek first the kingdom of God and His righteousness, and all these *things* will be added unto you"—(if we need them).

Sixth Day.

Matthew 9:2; John 16:33; Acts 23:11: 2 And behold, they brought to him a man sick of the palsy, lying on a bed: And Jesus seeing their faith said unto the sick of the palsy, Son, *be of good cheer;* thy sins are forgiven. 33 These things have I spoken unto you, that in me ye may have peace. In the world ye have tribulation: but *be of good cheer;* I have overcome the world. 11 And the night following the Lord stood by him, and said, *Be of good cheer:* for as thou hast testified concerning me at Jerusalem, so must thou bear witness also at Rome.

Please mark the times and places where the expression "be of good cheer" appears. What would you say to our Lord if you were sick of palsy and He told you to be of good cheer because your sins were forgiven? What possible connection is there between palsy and forgiveness of sins? It would be easier to answer this question than to say how "good cheer" relates to the forgiveness of sins. Where is the estatic happiness; the solid contentment we should have because our sins are forgiven? Let's look at this experience from our Lord's viewpoint—Jesus was full of "good cheer"—why? because He was involved in the happy experience of forgiving sins! We too can share in pointing men to the Lamb of God who taketh away sin—does this elicit an emotional charge from us?—or at least a deep feeling of satisfaction?—honestly now does it?

Where and when did Jesus overcome the world? Wait a moment before you answer—answer this from your point of view—is not the world—its demands and allurements still a very real part of your daily experience? How then can we be of "good cheer"? In what way has Jesus overcome the world for me? Our past sins are forgiven, but what of the present power of sin today? Did Jesus fail in His purpose, or have we failed in appropriating? Let's kneel before Him and ask not only for cleansing from sin but a presence within to enable us to overcome.

Jesus said Paul was to be of "good cheer" in the knowledge of Jesus' personal interest in the decisions of every day. No opposition—no refusal—no misunderstanding happened in Paul's experience without the personal interest of our Lord. And not only so—but He was doing something about it—Jesus was in control of every changing circumstance and would finally bring Paul to Rome and make of him there a witness for Him. Does Jesus have less interest in anyone of us?—The good Shepherd would lay down His life for anyone of His lost sheep—does this bring any cheer to our hearts?

Seventh Day.

Matthew 9:10-15: And it came to pass, as he sat at meat in the house, behold, many publicans and sinners came and sat down with Jesus and his disciples. And when the Pharisees saw it, they said unto his disciples, Why eateth your Teacher with the publicans and sinners? But when he heard it, he said, They that are whole have no need of a physician, but they that are sick. But go ye and learn what this meaneth, I desire mercy, and not sacrifice: for I came not to call the righteous, but sinners. Then came to him the disciples of John, saying, Why do we and the Pharisees fast oft, but thy disciples fast not? And Jesus said unto them, Can the sons of the bridechamber mourn, as long as the bridegroom is with them? but the days will come, when the bridegroom shall be taken away from them, and then will they fast.

Our Lord said the He and His disciples were as happy as "a bridal party on a honeymoon"! This was the satisfaction and happiness that filled His heart in relation to His work.

The bridegroom is not with us today as He was in the days of His flesh—but He is with us—even as He said (Matt. 28:20) —we are the "sons of the bride chamber"—we are engaged in the happy task of introducing the bridegroom to His potential bride—with such a worthy bridegroom this should be a happy privilege!

Comment For The Week
THE MASTER'S JOY

Whereas I surely do not concur with some other writings of the following author his words on *"The Master's Joy"* are greatly appreciated:

The New Testament is the most joyful book in the world. It opens with joy over the birth of Jesus; and it ends with a superb picture of a multitude which no man could number, singing Hallelujah Choruses. No matter where you open it, amid fortunate or discouraging circumstances, you always hear a note of joy. Even when a company of friends gather at a farewell supper, before their Leader is crucified, he says to them, "These things have I spoken unto you, that my joy may be in you, and that your joy may be made full" (John 15:11). Even when their best friend has gone, the mourners take "their food with gladness, and singleness of heart, praising God" (Acts 2:46). They therefore departed from the presence of the council, rejoicing that they were "counted worthy to suffer dishonor for the Name" (Acts 5:41); when an apostle is put in jail overnight he passes the time singing (Acts 16:25), and if you listen to him in his Roman prison, you will hear him dictating, "Rejoice in the Lord always: again I will say, Rejoice" (Phil. 4:4). There is enough tragedy in the New Testament to make it the saddest book in the world, and instead it is the joyfullest.

The religion which expresses itself in this book and which issues from it, is the most joyful religion on earth. Three great missionary faiths are in existence today: Mohammedanism, Buddhism, Christianity. The first has no hymns and never sings. The second is only now endeavoring to compete with Christianity by copying our songs. Here is a speciman of Buddhist plagiarism:

> "O for a thousand tongues to sing
> My holy Buddha's praise:
> The glories of my teacher great,
> The triumphs of his grace!
> Buddha! the name that kills our fears,
> That bids our sorrows cease:
> 'Tis music in the speaker's ears,
> 'This life, and health, and peace.

> Hear him, ye deaf; his praise, ye dumb,
>> Your loosened tongues employ;
> Ye blind, behold your Buddha come;
>> And leap, ye lame, for joy."

So Buddhism endeavors to graft into her pessimistic thought of life a little of that radiant hymnology in which sixty generations of Christians spontaneously have broken into song.

Behind this joyous book and this joyous religion stands a joyful personality. The mournful pictures of him in mediæval art are proved to be wrong by the records of his life and the consequences of his influence. The most joyous religion and book in existence were not inspired by a melancholy man. Swinburne, missing the mark as usual, sings of him:

> "Thou has conquered, O pale Galilean,
> The world has grown grey with thy breath!"

Was Jesus a "pale Galilean"? Has the world "grown grey with his breath"? Let us look at him and see.

On the two occasions when Jesus took special pains to justify his conduct to his enemies, he was explaining to them why he and his disciples were so joyful. In Mark 2:18,19, he is justifying the refusal of his little company to fast. A Pharisee fasted twice every week, on Mondays and Thursdays, whether he felt like it or not. Jesus says that insincere, forced abstinence is useless, and that he and his disciples are as happy as a bridal party and do not wish to fast. This is a skillful way of putting the matter, because, according to the Jewish law, a bridal party was always exempt from fasting. Jesus claims that he and his friends are on a continuous honeymoon, and that the Pharisaic laws have no right to interrupt their freedom.

On another occasion the Pharisees complain because he welcomes sinners to his friendship. He tells them (Luke 15) that the work which he is doing in finding lost men and bringing them back to their true life, is the joyfullest work in the world. He says that he is as glad over it as a shepherd who calls in his neighbors for a feast when a lost sheep is rescued; as full of satisfaction as a housewife who has lost a coin and found it; as happy as a father whose prodigal son has come home. He says that this sort of experience which he is enjoying makes the angels sing, and that such joy he will not exchange for the exclusiveness of the Pharisees.

Jesus was so joyful in his *friendships* and his *work* that he fairly was forced to defend himself, on account of it, before his enemies. The reason for Jesus' joyfulness corresponds to a universal law that the happiest people on earth are those who are doing most for others. We say that Jesus' earthly life was the time of his humiliation and self-sacrifice, but when he speaks of it, he says in joy, "My meat is to do the will of him that sent me." He loves his life. Take him at his most disheartened day, when hostility assails him and friends desert, yet you feel that nothing could buy him off or woo him away from the work of service which he is doing. He loves, it, glories in it, would be miserable if deprived of it. He finds life by losing it (Matt. 10:39), and defines greatness in terms of usefulness (Matt. 20:25-28). We smaller souls, when for the sake of greater good we surrender a lesser convenience, fix our thoughts and settle our remembrance on the sacrifice which we have made. But Jesus said that a man found a treasure in a field, and in his joy sold all that he had and bought that field(Matt. 13:44). The emphasis of Jesus is not upon the sacrifice, but upon the joy of finding the spiritual treasure and getting it at any price. Only in great souls do you find to the full this joy in service. It is in Paul when, amid his tremendous hardships, he says, "We also rejoice in our tribulations." It is in David Livingstone, who after his terrible sufferings in Africa said, "I never made a sacrifice in my life." They felt about their work for others what Nelson felt about war, when at Aboukir, with the shot and splinters from the deck flying all about him, he said: "This is warm work and it may be the last of us at any minute," and then, as he turned away, "but I wouldn't be elsewhere for thousands!"

Another reason for this exultant spirit in Jesus is also fundamental. He had the most·joyous idea of God that ever was thought of. He taught his disciples that they could take the most beautiful aspects of human life, like fatherhood, and lifting them up to the best they could imagine, could say, God is much better than this. "If ye then, being evil," he said, "know how to give good gifts unto your children, how much more shall your Father"

(Matt. 7:11). This is the most joyous thought of God of which
we know. For centuries men had enthroned in heaven their evil
with their good, their jealousies, even their lusts and passions.
Jesus taught men to interpret God in terms of the spiritually best
they could imagine. Whatsoever things are just, true, honorable,
pure, lovely, and of good report, if there way any virtue and
any praise, Jesus affirmed these things of God.

When a scientist catches this method of Jesus in thinking of
God, he says in the words of Sir Oliver Lodge of the University
of Manchester, "I will not believe that it is given to man to
have thoughts, higher and nobler than the real truth of things."
When a poet takes fire from Jesus' joyful conception of God,
he pictures, as Browning does in "Saul," a man longing to help
his friend, and then pictures him rising from this human love
toward God to cry:

"Would I suffer for him that I love? So wouldst thou—
        so wilt thou!
So shall crown thee life's topmost, ineffablest, uttermost crown—
And thy love fill infinitude wholly, nor leave up nor down
One spot for the creature to stand in!"

This thought of God is peculiarly Jesus' contribution to the world,
and no other ever compared with it in joyousness. It stands to
reason that no gloomy soul ever really held, much less originated such a jubilant conception of Deity.

Out of this thought of God a boundless hope inevitably comes.
Because God is unimaginably good, "exceeding abundantly above
all we can ask or think," nothing is too good to be true. If three
quarters of Jesus' work falls on poor ground and is lost, Jesus
is sure that one quarter will come to glorious fruition (Matt.
13:1ff). If his cause is very meager in its beginnings, he has
no doubt that it will grow to a great outcome like a mustard
seed becoming a tree, or leaven fermenting the entire pan of
dough (Matt. 13:31ff). If tares and wheat are seen competing
in the field of the world, Jesus never suspects that the tares will
win the victory; he knows the wheat will (Matt. 13:24-30).
When his enemies grow menacing and his disciples are frightened,
Jesus' hope never wavers: "Every plant which my heavenly
Father planted not shall be rooted up. Let them alone" (Matt.
15:13,14). Jesus was perfectly sure of the victory of right over

wrong. In this sense he was profoundly an optimist. It is absurd to suppose that a sad soul could hold such an undiscourageable and jubilant hope as this.

The gospels show clearly that this joyousness of Jesus overflowed in all the familiar ways that everywhere are the signs of a radiant nature. When his enemies says that he was "a gluttonous man and a wine bibber" (Matt. 11:19), it is a gross slander, but it is clear that such an accusation would not have gained currency, unless, like his first disciples, he had taken his food with gladness. None but a joyful soul loves children as Jesus did and finds in their artless and care-free company a solace and delight (Mark 10:16). None but a joyful soul loves nature as Jesus did, watching the changing weather signals of an evening sky in summer (Matt. 16:2,3), or considering the lilies, how they grow, more beautiful than Solomon in all his glory (Matt. 6:28,29). None but a joyful soul could have shed over his teaching, as serious teaching as there is in the race's history, such a spontaneous play of good humor as Jesus uses. He never jests as Socrates does, but he often lets the ripple of a happy breeze play over the surface of his mighty deep. When he is teaching the disciples the necessity of patient and persistent prayer, he describes the appearance of God to the impatient man as that of a sulky neighbor in bed with his children who will not readily get up and open the door (Luke 11:5-8). When he wishes to picture the meanness of an unforgiving spirit, he tells of a servant who had just been forgiven a debt of $12,-000,000, but who went out and choked a fellow-servant who owed him $17 (Matt. 18:23-35). When he wishes to reprove harsh judgment on the part of a man who forgets his own sins, he pictures a man with a beam in his own eye, painfully squinting to get a mote from the eye of his brother (Matt. 7:2,3). This reminds one of Confucius' whimsical simile: "Let every man sweep the snow from his own doors, and not trouble himself about the hoarfrost on his neighbor's tiles." When Jesus deals with people who are sick, sinful, wretched, his common exclamation is "Be of good cheer!" Even after he has left the earth, Paul dreaming of him, hears him say, as though it were his characteristic utterance, "Be of good cheer" (Acts 23:11). There are times when Jesus is burdened, times even when he abstains from food and gives himself to solitary prayer, but he must in all such cases have followed his own admonition to his disciples: "When ye fast, be not, as the hypocrites, of a sad countenance: . . . but thou, when thou fastest, anoint thy head, and wash thy face; that thou be not seen of men to fast" (Matt. 6:16-18). Jesus must have been the most radiant man to be found in his day in Palestine. He must have carried with him an atmosphere of glad good-will. Like springs of fresh water by the sea, even when the salt waves of sorrow went over him, he must have come up again with inexhaustible kindliness and joy. What the gospels report once, must have been his characteristic effect on all who loved him, "Then were the disciples glad when they saw the Lord."

At first, this representation of the Master may seem to deny one of the most fundamental truths about him, that "he was a man of sorrows and acquainted with grief." The interpretation of Jesus' character in art and in ordinary thought has depended largely on his cries of agony: "Now is my soul troubled; and what shall I say?" (John 12:27); "My soul is exceeding sorrowful even unto death" (Mark 14:34). There is, however, no conflict between Jesus, "the man of sorrows," and Jesus, the man of joy. Joy and sorrow are not alien and antagonistic; they both come from the same capacity for feeling, the same breadth of sensitive surface which the soul exposes to the touch of God and of the world.

"He who lives more lives than one,
    More deaths than one must die."

The ocean that has sweep and depth in it for sea-going tempests, has room for calms also, with a verge and horizon to their peace that no pool can know. The place where great storms arise is the place where great calms fall. The same capacity is required by both. A man of deep sorrows and deep joys must always be the same man—with what a range and depth of feeling! Jesus is so glad in communion with his Father, that on a mountain top his very face is transfigured; and he is so broken-hearted in Gethsemane that his brow sweats blood. When he is sorrowful, no sorrow is like his ;and when he is joyful, what a sweep of water and depth of sky for his gladness!

71

Indeed, the impression of Jesus' joyousness is greater because of his sorrows. Jesus had been the real encourager of men because his joy sustained the shock of cruel circumstance and agonizing struggle and came off victorious. Like a rainbow, his gladness often gets part of its effect because it is built on the clouds of a preceding storm. When his trouble was at its climax in the upper room at the last supper his joy was unquenched. "Be of good cheer," he said, "I have overcome the world." The men who have most cheered their fellows are not the men of untroubled lives, but those whose spirits were too glad to be submerged by sorrow. Robert Louis Stevenson, exiled to Samoa for his health, and sure to die there soon, prayed, "Give us to awaken with smiles give us to labor smiling; and as the sun lightens the world, so let our loving-kindness make bright this house of our habitation." Such men have been the joy-bringers of the race, and Jesus is the Master of them.

This is the most significant fact about Jesus' joy, that the sources of it were not at the mercy of men and circumstance. There were sources of gladness in Jesus' life which were dependent on the good-will of men. His satisfaction in the creature-comforts of life, his delight in the free and unimpeded teaching of the people, his confidence in his disciples, including Judas—these and other doors of joy in the Master's experience, were at the mercy of men. And they closed them. All through the final months of his ministry you can hear the click of closing doors around his life, until at last they shut him into the upper room to face a terrible tomorrow. Every door which the hand of man could reach was closed. Then that wonderful thing happened, which is the mark of all exalted souls and supremely of the Master; he fell back on resources which the hand of man could not touch. "My joy I give unto you," he said, "and your joy no man taketh from you." Jesus' blessedness was not like a brook that flows from melting snow which can be made to vanish by the sun, but like a stream that has exhaustless springs to draw from. He could stand anything that men or circumstances could do to him and still have resources of joy. He was an unconquerable soul. He even told his disciples that when they were persecuted, they could still "rejoice and be exceeding glad" (Matt. 5:12).

Whatever else may be true of Jesus, he was no "pale Galilean." The first impression which he makes is one of overflowing radiance and gladness. (THE MANHOOD OF THE MASTER pp. 11-18)

THE FRUIT OF THE SPIRIT IS PEACE

May the peace of God guard your heart and your thoughts. Who is the "Prince of Peace"? To have the presence of Him through His Holy Spirit is to have peace. Indeed, "He is our peace."

First Day.

Philippians 4:6,7: In nothing be anxious; but in everything by prayer and supplication with thanksgiving let your requests be made known unto God. And the peace of God, which passeth all understanding, shall guard your hearts and your thoughts in Christ Jesus.

It might be well to read from verse four of the fourth chapter of Philippians, "Rejoice in the Lord always; again I will say, Rejoice. Let your forbearance (gentleness) be known unto all men. The Lord is at hand." We could call verses 4 thru 6 the preliminaries to peace. Notice them: (1) "Rejoice in the Lord always"—this is only possible when we believe the Lord is interested in and a part of every changing circumstance of life. When the Lord is *in* every part of our daily life we can rejoice in the knowledge that it is up to Him not up to us, to bring out of the circumstance what He wants not what we want. We can rejoice because we know He is working together all the parts for our good.

(2) "Let your forbearance or gentleness be known (advertised) to all men (—how?)—by what means?—*"The Lord is at hand"*—We can relax in the Lord and offer to all men a demeanor of gentleness when we know Jesus stands at our side (invisible but none-the-less there). "The Lord is at hand" to forgive—to hear our prayer—to strengthen our inward man by His Spirit—He cannot help if we do not ask Him—but He is there for this purpose.

(3) "In nothing be anxious; but in everything by prayer and supplication with thanksgiving let your requests be made known unto God." The great enemy of peace (anxiety) is defeated by prayer—supplication, and thanksgiving. Notice the delineation

here: (1) Prayer—i.e. general requests, (2) Supplication—i.e. specific requests, (3) To pray and make supplication with a confidence that God is more interested in answering and helping than you are in asking—this will give you a great sense of thanksgiving for the answer is already on the way.

Now we are ready to enjoy the peace of God—mark the conjunction "and" which begins verse seven—"And the peace of God, which passeth all understanding, shall guard your heart (emotional nature) and your thoughts (intellectual nature) in Christ Jesus." This is true *only if* the preliminary preparations are made—*only if:* (1) We rejoice in the Lord always because the Lord controls all, (2) We offer a constant, gentle demeanor to the world because the Lord is at hand to help, (3) If we pray and make supplication about our frustrations with absolute confidence in the Lord's personal interest in such matters—THEN the peace of God will garrison our hearts and thoughts. This our Lord did. This we can and must do to have peace.

Second Day.

John 14:1-3: Let not your heart be troubled: believe in God, believe also in me. In my Father's house are many mansions; if it were not so, I would have told you; for I go to prepare a place for you. And if I go and prepare a place for you, I come again, and will receive you unto myself; that where I am, there ye may be also.

Peace comes when we are able to fasten our hopes upon a time when the enemies of peace will be removed and we will be able to enjoy tranquility. If in the midst of conflict there is no hope for release or removal peace is impossible.

Life is a conflict—a battle—but it will one day be over—there will be a new life—a new world—there *is* the Father's house of many mansions. To hold this thought before us—to meditate upon it in the midst the fight is to provide a secret source of peace—"Light and life cometh in the morning." This hope can and does give peace. Once again we must say that such a hope of heaven must be sure and steadfast—it can not be a sentimental wish—such will not give peace—Jesus had no hesitancy in His hope of heaven—this gave Him peace. The presence of the Father was a constant reality to our Lord and so was the assurance and prospect of the world and life to come. In His imagination He could live in another WORLD—and have peace. We are but pilgrims here—our real cause is in another land—in another WORLD—in that "upper and better kingdom"—in our imagination we can even in the midst of frustrations look up and for a moment live "in the WORLD to come" and have strength and peace to face the life that now is.

Third Day.

John 14:27: Peace I leave with you; my peace I give unto you: not as the world giveth, give I unto you. Let not your heart be troubled, neither let it be fearful.

Let's begin this study with a series of probing questions—questions for the heart:

1. Specifically what is the peace Jesus has left with us?
2. Why speak of leaving His peace, was it something He could not give until He left?
3. Why call it His peace ("My peace")? Is this in contrast to others?
4. Can the world give some form or kind of peace? What is the meaning of the little phrase, "not as the world giveth, give I unto you."
5. What was the particular area of trouble when Jesus said "Let not your heart be troubled"?

1. In answer to the first question there are at least three answers to this query, and all of them correct:
   A. Jesus has left us the wonderful peace attendant in the forgiveness of all our past sins—in a very real sense this is the peace belonging to and purchased by our Lord, given to us—this is what Paul meant when he said, "He is our peace." (Eph. 2:14).
   B. Jesus brings peace when He moves into our hearts and our conscience through His wonderful gift the Holy Spirit—The fruit of the Spirit's indwelling is peace. This too is His particular possession purchased at such a great price—His own blood!
   C. The final and eternal peace in the Father's house is also a real possibility.

75

To encompass the three aspects of peace in a personal experience in daily living is what we want and what our Lord promised.

2. Why speak of *leaving* His peace? It was because He did not wish to leave His disciples in a troubled state of heart—while He was with them they had peace—when their peace was disturbed they could come to Him for an answer to their problems. He wanted them to have a constant continuing peace. The great peacemaker is the Holy Spirit—the continuing Christ—let the Holy Spirit do now what Jesus did for His disciples when He was with them. He has council and comfort to give us. Jesus had left to sit down at the right hand of the Father and has sent the Holy Comforter into our hearts to bring us peace.

3. All other offers of peace are empty—"There is no peace saith my God to the wicked." There is no source of peace but Jesus—this is why He could refer to this as "my peace." In this troubled, frustrated, neurotic life we do indeed need peace of mind, but we can not find it in the wisdom of men—"it is not in man to direct his steps"—neither is it in him to provide peace. We are out of tune with God first and then our fellowmen. Jesus is our peace with God and with each man.

4. The world can and does offer a form of peace either in a pill or prescription of some type—all such efforts are temporary and incomplete. Jesus makes no such offer, all those who have come to Jesus to ask for "rest for their souls" have found it. Not a few could say of the rest they have found: "Not as the world" is my rest and peace in God thru Christ!

5. The apostles were concerned about the departure of Jesus—Jesus was about to return to the Father—they felt they would be left desolate and for this reason were troubled. Jesus reminded them that even though He was leaving He was not leaving them—He would yet be with them in the presence and person of the blessed Holy Spirit—in this they could have peace.

Fourth Day.

Luke 11:2a: And he said unto them, when ye pray, say, Our Father which art in Heaven, *Hallowed be thy name* ...

"The fear of the Lord is the beginning of wisdom." (Prov. 9:10)

76

The fear of the Lord is not only the beginning of wisdom but the beginning of peace.

There is nothing wrong with fear itself. Fear apart from the objects toward which it is directed is "heaven sent" and a God given" inherent quality of God's creation—man. On the streets of a modern city the "fearless man" if the phrase were to be taken literally would be either dead or dying by nightfall. Jesus knew from the beginning that fear is both necessary and useful— He had His fear directed toward the right thing—hence everything else was right. Was Jesus ever afraid of men and what they could do or say against Him? Of course He was—He was tempted in all points like as we are tempted. He must have felt the icy fingers of fear and anxiety around his heart as He saw the officials talking and planning together to slay Him—to deceive Him, to lie about Him. But—He feared God more! The result of overpowering fear of man or circumstance is to give in to it. What would be the inevitable result of fearing God in the same manner? If we hallow the presence and authority of God more than man we will have *peace* with God! Why? Because we allow God to dominate our thoughts and actions. Peace is the result of the indwelling of the God of peace—this must and does come about through our deliberate choice!

Fifth Day.

"Thou wilt keep Him in perfect peace whose mind is stayed on thee . . ." (Isaiah 26:3)

The mind and face of our Lord was constantly set on His heavenly Father. Because of this Jesus faced up squarely to every fearful circumstance and *faced it down.* This is the only road to peace.

Jesus knew the censure of going through Samaria—did this keep Him out?

Jesus knew the Jews had no dealings with the Samaritans and especially women Samaritans—did this prevent Him from speaking to the poor lost woman at the well?

Jesus knew that the Jews would criticize Him for healing on the Sabbath, Jesus knew it wasn't socially acceptable to eat with publicans and sinners—but in every circumstance He feared God (reverenced God) more than man and therefore faced down such fears and had peace. We need to know as our Lord did that dangerous situations are not necessarily undesirable. They can provide a growth in character that nothing else could. Jesus taught us that we learn and earn peace by the things we suffer, but not unless our mind—or heart—our purpose is set upon God's will and not man's.

Sixth Day.

Matt. 6:25-30: Therefore I say unto you, Be not anxious for your life, what ye shall eat, or what ye shall drink; nor yet for your body, what ye shall put on. Is not the life more than the food, and the body more than the raiment? Behold the birds of the heaven, that they sow not, neither do they reap, nor gather into barns; and your heavenly Father feedeth them. Are not ye of much more value than they? And which of you by being anxious can add one cubit unto the measure of his life? And why are ye anxious concerning raiment? Consider the lilies of the field, how they grow; they toil not, neither do they spin: yet Solomon in all his glory was not arrayed like one of these. But if God doth so clothe the grass of the field, which to-day is, and to-morrow is cast into the oven, shall he not much more clothe you, O ye of little faith?

Jesus never misused His imagination concerning His fears and therefore had peace. This is just another way of saying our Lord never crossed any bridges before He came to them. Jesus never laid awake nights conjuring up a trial before it came to Him. But, "someone says, that is hardly a fair comparison—Jesus had the foreknowledge of God." Yes, *and so do you!* Read it: "No temptation (trial) shall take you but what is common to man, but God is faithful, who will not suffer you to be tempted above what ye are able to bear." You have this foreknowledge of God's unfailing promise, why worry and destroy your peace?

Our picture making capacity can fill our minds with visual images of disasters possible and impossible, until many of us spend our lives bearing troubles, most of which never happened. "Our imaginary worry may be unreal, but the worried imagination is very real"—and so is the complete absence of peace. Most of us can exercise a considerable measure of control over our imagination, indeed, by the Spirit of God we can "bring every thought into captivity unto Christ Jesus." We can all recognize the pet reels of moving pictures we habitually run through our minds to stimulate anxiety. We are so much like the cowboy who went to his first western movie—he became enraged at the villain on the screen and began shooting at the figure on the screen instad of the projector where they originated. So we, tormented by creatures of our imagination center our attention on the mental screen where their visual procession moves rather than on the inner faculty where we ourselves project these obsessive, abhorred, and yet self-centered fantasies. Change the reels, run one on Abraham, Noah, one on the sparrow or the lily! God, give us "the mind of Christ"!

Seventh Day.

He that covereth his sins shall not prosper: but whoso confesseth and forsaketh them shall have mercy." (and therefore peace) Prov. 28:13.

Some people have no peace because they have covered their sins. Jesus knew nothing of this and neither should we. The poet so well said:

"I have to live with myself, and so
　I want to be fit for myself to know;
I want to be able as the days go by,
　Always to look myself straight in the eye.
I do not want to stand with the setting of the sun,
　And hate myself for the things I have done."

or once again—

"I digged a grave and laid within its secret depths one
　secret sin;
I closed the grave—but now I know full well—that day
　I shut myself in Hell!"

"There is no peace saith my God to the wicked." (Is. 57:21)

Clean out your heart and a deep peace will settle over your whole being.

Comment For The Week
PEACE
L. E. Maxwell
On earth peace, good will toward men.
　　　　　—Luke 2:14

To General Douglas MacArthur on Wake Island in 1950 President Truman said, "I want only three words as my epitaph

—'He Brought Peace'." What a worthy and noble ambition! Yet how delusive and disappointing the hope! How can there be world peace with no basis, with no foundation? What kind of peace can man build upon the boundless greed and white-hot passions of sinful humanity? If the Prince of Peace Himself cannot promote a peace among such sinning men and nations, how could the politician from the Pendergast party of Kansas City hope to win as his epitaph, "He Brought Peace"? Perhaps he only expressed the desperation of a decadent leadership. We are reminded of Prime Minister Chamberlain's hurried appeasement of Herr Hitler, when he brought back his "Peace with Honour."

Christianity Questioned

There is a growing skepticism and practical atheism among many leaders of today. While there are touches of real revival here and there in foreign fields—the increased religious interest in North America is perhaps largely a revival of Churchianity—there is developing in so-called Christendom an intellectual infidelity of the deepest dye. Whereas our political leadership of fifty years ago hoped that the Christian religion would gradually bring in the Millennium, present day men are for the most part skeptical. To them Christianity has failed, failed as a practical solution to the world's problems. They feel that if, after two thousand years of Christianity (the religion of peace) the world faces greater problems and greater dangers than ever before, then the angelic proclamation of "peace on earth" must be discarded, and relegated to the land of limbo along with all the religious superstitions of all the ages.

It is not surprising that well meaning people, those who have never met the living Christ in saving experience, should be deeply confirmed in this general infidelity. Their reasoning sums up to something like this: Since the Christian way of life is so widely rejected—"few there be that find it"—then Messianic deliverance through this other-worldly message is, in the face of A-Bombs, H-Bombs, food shortages, and world tensions, only a pious aspiration, a mere mockery void of all practical application in such a world as ours.

Peace Twofold

To the men of this troubled world whose only hope is "under the sun" it may seem like an age-long bit of superstition to sing year after year the song of the heavenly hosts:

Glory to God in the highest,
And on earth peace, good will
toward men.

Glory to God in the highest—that may be very well. But on earth, what? Peace! Peace? What kind of peace? Peace indeed. But where? Only "among men in whom He is well pleased."

Leaders of all nations talk peace. Men everywhere are trying to produce peace, a peace based upon "good will" and understanding. But peace among men depends upon peace with God. Peace is twofold, first heavenward and then manward. Man therefore needs a double reconciliation, first with God and then with his fellow man. Peace is found "among men in whom He is well pleased."

Need of Peace with God

The troubled and turbulent seas of wicked humanity cannot rest. The explosive vices, the moral corruptions, the guilty consciences, the fierce passions—these all cast up mire and dirt. There is no peace to the wicked. The deep need of man everywhere is peace, peace with God.

It is this need of peace that reveals man's vast and pressing need for reconciliation. Man is an enemy, an exile, a rebel, and it is this wilful rejection of God—His love, His claims, His truth, His dominion—that is the root cause of all the world's woes. How can the unreconciled sinner, the fugitive from justice, the rebel against his King—how, I ask, can such a man be at peace, either with God or with man?

If the dull and stupid conscience of man could be quickened to feel and express its first and deepest need, it would re-echo the publican's cry, God be merciful, God be propitious, God be reconciled to me, a sinner.

A poor dying woman once expressed the inner agony of every soul under the guilt and condemnation of sin. Utterly ignorant of the way of peace and without the least knowledge of the Christian faith, the poor soul voiced the need universal when

81

she cried, "Oh that it were possible for someone to take my guilty conscience as it were his own, that I might find a little peace!" Of course that is just the cause of the Saviour's coming into the world; just why Christ went to the Cross. God made Him who knew no sin to be sin for us, taking our guilty conscience as it were His own and suffering for sins, the Just for the unjust, that He might bring us to God. He "made peace by the Blood of His Cross."

Jehovah bade His sword awake,
O Christ, it woke 'gainst Thee;
Thy blood the flaming blade must slake,
Thy heart its sheath must be.
All for my sake, my peace to make;
Now sleeps that sword for me.

Peace Among Men

The reconciled rebel, having found peace with God, knows the meaning of "peace on earth, peace among men of His good pleasure" (Morgan). He has found the foundation, the only basis of peace on earth, namely, peace with God.

This gospel of reconciliation promotes peace among men. We dare not minimize the social effects of Christ's advent into our sinful world. God came in Christ reconciling the world unto Himself. Now His reconciled followers are "the salt of the earth," preserving, flavoring, influencing for good; "the light of the world," burning and shining and dispelling darkness. Who can measure the influence of old-time gospel work to convict of sin and solve the sin problem? Mighty emancipations have been effected, such as setting free the slaves, exalting womanhood, and promoting scores of peace-making agencies for the relief of the sick, the burdened, and the oppressed. Yet all these ameliorating influences are but the by-products of Christ's first advent into the world. It is reconciliation with God that promotes peace among men.

Peace Among Ourselves

How important is "peace among men of His good pleasure!" In His work on the Cross Christ not only made peace between man and God, but also between man and man. Therefore let us as believers, "have peace one with another."

How Can I Have the Fruit of the Spirit?

The Jew and the Gentile of Christ's day represented the greatest extremes of race and religion. Just when that enmity was at its height, and the most inveterate and desperate that anyone could conceive, an enmity representative of all that divides and separates mankind—just at such a time Paul declares that in Christ who "is our peace" the middle wall of partition has been broken down. There is neither Jew nor Greek, for Christ has created "in Himself of twain one new man, so making peace" (Eph. 2:15). Adolf Monod of France said, "Behold the secret of all true union! It is not by others coming to us, nor by our going over to them; but it is by both them and ourselves coming to Christ" that peace is made.

In this day of growing division—the accusation of Scripture still stands, "Are ye not carnal?"—let us carefully and firmly seek to pull down and keep down all partitions, all walls, all barriers among the members of Christ's body. "Endeavoring to keep the unity of the Spirit"—Christ made it; we are to keep it—"in the bond of peace . . . till we all come into the unity of the faith, and of the knowledge of the Son of God, unto a perfect man." Paul says division is a sign of carnality, of ignorance and ungrown-upness—a proof of babyhood. Let us prayerfully and humbly hold out for unity in the "one body" of which Christ is "The Head"—till we grow up. Then we shall the better understand the Christmas "peace on earth, peace among men of His good pleasure." ABANDONED TO CHRIST—L. E. Maxwell, pp. 90-94.

THE FRUIT OF THE SPIRIT IS LONGSUFFERING

Our Lord is and was the living example of this virtue. To be like Jesus is to be filled with longsuffering—this we can never be without Divine aid—the help in the inward man of the blessed Holy Spirit. Shall we study the life of our Lord in the area of longsuffering and ask (yea-permit) the Holy Spirit to translate this into our life?

First Day.

I Peter 2:20, 21: For what glory is it, if, when ye sin, and are buffeted for it, ye shall take it patiently? but if, when ye do well, and suffer for it, ye shall take it patiently, this is acceptable with God. For hereunto were ye called: because

Christ also suffered for you, leaving you an example, that ye should follow in His steps:

There can be no longsuffering without suffering. We would all like to have this wonderful quality of longsuffering if we could just obtain it minus the suffering. It is like humility—we would all be happy to be humble if it were not connected with humiliation—we want to have humility without humiliation—longsuffering with no suffering—it will not be! Peter offers a very real circumstance in which the longsuffering of our Lord was demonstrated—you are the body of Christ are you not? i.e. We together make up His present body on earth. When was the last time you were lied about—mistreated in job promotion—misrepresented in motive for doing good? How did you take it?—patiently like Jesus in Pilate's hall? If our Lord left us an example in longsuffering we can be sure it was because He wanted us to follow it and *because it is possible to do so!* Not humanly possible—but by His Spirit we can and will follow Him—yea—share in His suffering in the manner He first suffered for us. We suffer for Him because He first suffered for us.

Second Day.

Matthew 12:41, 42: The men of Nineveh shall stand up in the judgment with this generation, and shall condemn it: for they repented at the preaching of Jonah; and behold, a greater than Jonah is here. The queen of the south shall rise up in the judgment with this generation, and shall condemn it: for she came from the ends of the earth to hear the wisdom of Solomon; and behold, a greater than Solomon is here.

Are you tempted to whine—and to pity yourself when men do not repent at your preaching? All men did not repent at the preaching of Jesus—it was not because they did not understand or that the message was not appropriate (as is sometimes the case with us) but men *did not* repent. Have you felt (like all of us have at times) you were engaged in the "pearl casting business," and most who received your words were swine? What would it mean to be a greater than Solomon and then be rejected? —do we see or hear of any impatience from Jesus? What can our so-called "jewels of wisdom" be in comparison with what He taught? Have you ever been bothered by the apparent success of a fellow preacher (perhaps preaching in Nineveh)? He can report almost twice the number of conversions per year—you know—and have been told by others that you are in every way a greater preacher than the fellow over in Nineveh—but men do not repent at your preaching—what do you do? React like Jesus?—can we bear patiently when we remember our Lord was greater than Jonah—or anyone else who ever spoke and men did not repent at His word? There was no resentment in His heart because He was sure "no word of God was void of power" —it would accomplish what God wanted—and this He wanted.

Third Day.

Mark 10:35-41: And there come near unto him James and John, the sons of Zebedee, saying unto him, Teacher, we would that thou shouldest do for us whatsoever we shall ask of thee. And he said unto them, What would ye that I should do for you? And they said unto him, Grant unto us that we may sit, one on thy right hand, and one on thy left hand, in thy glory. But Jesus said unto them, Ye know not what ye ask. Are ye able to drink the cup that I drink? or to be baptized with the baptism that I am baptized with? And they said unto him, We are able. And Jesus said unto them, The cup that I drink ye shall drink; and with the baptism that I am baptized withal shall ye be baptized: but to sit on my right hand or on my left hand is not mine to give; but it is for them for whom it hath been prepared. And when the ten heard it, they began to be moved with indignation concerning James and John.

And there came unto him Tom and Melvin, two of the elders of the church where he preached—"Preacher," they said—"we have a very urgent and important request to make of you,"— "What is it boys?" he replied. "Just this—we want to head up the finance and pulpit committees of this church. We do not have enough money, and we believe some improvements could be made in the pulpit." What would the average preacher have in mind for Tom and Melvin?—What did Jesus plan for James and John? He would use them to build His church. Didn't the selfish ambition of these two apostles threaten the work of Christ? Of course it did, but He was longsuffering and willing to wait and to believe they would one day understand how foolish was their request. The patience of our Master helped Him to see and not discount the present work of Peter and John. He here called it "a cup and a baptism." Do your work now and God will show you—and all, who will help the finances and the pulpit hereafter. This is longsuffering in action!

Fourth Day.

Mark 14:32-42: And they come unto a place which was named Gethsemane: and he saith unto his disciples, Sit ye here, while I pray. And he taketh with him Peter and James and John, and began to be greatly amazed, and sore troubled. And he saith unto them, My soul is exceeding sorrowful even unto death: abide ye here, and watch. And he went forward a little, and fell on the ground, and prayed that, if it were possible, the hour might pass away from him. And he said, Abba, Father, all things are possible unto thee; remove this cup from me: howbeit not what I will, but what thou wilt. And he cometh, and findeth them sleeping, and saith unto Peter, Simon, sleepest thou? couldest thou not watch one hour? Watch and pray, that ye enter not into temptation: the spirit indeed is willing, but the flesh is weak. And again he went away, and prayed, saying the same words. And again he came, and found them sleeping, for their eyes were very heavy; and they knew not what to answer him. And he cometh the third time, and saith unto them, Sleep on now, and take your rest: it is enough; the hour is come; behold, the Son of man is betrayed into the hands of sinners. Arise, let us be going: behold, he that betrayeth me is at hand.

What one thing caused our Lord to suffer the most?—on a divine level it must have been the decision of Gethsemane—but on the human level the sleeping disciples must have cut Him most deeply. When those we love fail to share with us in our deepest need we are indeed sorely tempted to rebuke them and feel sorry for ourselves. When this happens once it is a keen disappointment—but to happen three times! "What—could you not watch with me one hour"?—but what was the rebuke?— "watch and pray, that ye enter not into temptation: the spirit is indeed willing, but the flesh is weak." Is there any indication of impatience? Far from impatience—He attempts to help Peter, James and John when they should have been a source of help to Him. Our Lord actually offers an explanation for the languor of the disciples—His apology was—"the spirit was to be somewhat blamed."—what amazing patience! Who was responsible for the actions of the inner man? The disciples were excusable only out of the unutterable love and grace of our Lord. Will we follow Him to Gethsemane in forgiving others as He did? Neither God's purpose nor our personal satisfaction are to be based upon what men do or do not do to us.

Fifth Day.

Mark 15:22-37: "And they bring him unto the place Golgotha, which is, being interpreted, The place of a skull. And they offered him wine mingled with myrrh: but he received it not. And they crucify him, and part his garments among them, casting lots upon them, what each should take. And it was the third hour, and they crucified him. And the superscription of his accusation was written over, THE KING OF THE JEWS. And with him they crucify two robbers; one on his right hand, and one on his left. And they that passed by railed on him, wagging their heads, and saying, Ha! thou that destroyest the temple, and buildest it in three days, save thyself, and come down from the cross. In like manner also the chief priests mocking him among themselves with the scribes said, He saved others; himself he cannot save. Let the Christ, the King of Israel, now come down from the cross, that we may see and believe. And they that were crucified with him reproached him. And when the sixth hour was come, there was darkness over the whole land until the ninth hour. And at the ninth hour Jesus cried with a loud voice, Eloi, Eloi, lama sabachthani? which is, being interpreted, My God, my God, why hast thou forsaken me? And some of them that stood by, when they heard it, said, Behold, he calleth Elijah. And one ran, and filling a sponge full of vinegar, put it on a reed, and gave him to drink, saying, Let be: let us see whether Elijah cometh to take him down. And Jesus uttered a loud voice, and gave up the ghost." Luke 23:34 "And Jesus said, Father, forgive them; for they know not what they do. And parting his garments among them, they cast lots."

Have you ever asked, "Why didn't they know what they were doing?" Was it because they did not have the opportunity to know? Was it because they did not want to know? —because they turned their back to the light and deliberately chose to walk into the darkness? Please notice that Jesus did not question the motive—it was enough for Him to know they did not know what they did. This is longsuffering in its highest expression. We many times are so full of our own plans that any rejections, any slighting (to say nothing of mocking or ridicule) will cause us to become exceedingly impatient. How did our Lord react in the interruption and rejection of His plans? In the upper room He stopped in the midst of giving the deep meaning of the last passover, to wash the feet of the disciples. While bearing the agony of the cross and the sins of the world He paused to pray for His murderers. This is longsuffering *with kindness.* I Cor. 13:4

Sixth Day.

John 12:23-25: "And Jesus answereth them, saying, The hour is come, that the Son of man should be glorified. Verily, verily, I say unto you, Except a grain of wheat fall into the earth and die, it abideth by itself alone; but if it dies, it beareth much fruit. He that loveth his life loseth it; and he that hateth his life in this world shall keep it unto life eternal."

We shall now discover the foundation of longsuffering—it is found in our Lord's attitude toward life. "He that loveth his life loseth it; and he that hateth his life in this world shall keep it unto life eternal." The object of the expression "loveth" as here used is in preference to society as we now know it—material, earthly, sensual life—the life that "consisteth in the abundance of *things*" in our present circumstance; a new car, a color T.V., a new home, new clothes, etc. Both poise and peace are lost in this material pursuit. When our time and talents are devoted to a running after "righteousness, godliness, faith, love, patience, meekness" (I Tim. 6:11) we find *in the race* the life, the peace, joy, hope, purpose, satisfaction we wanted and lost in the mad scramble for material gain. Do we believe this in theory or in fact? So many times we can say with our Lord, "Now is my soul troubled;" —but can we complete the thought with Him? "And what shall I say? Father save me from this hour (?) *But for this cause came I unto this hour.* Father, glorify thy name."

Seventh Day.

II Corinthians 4:7-10: "But we have this treasure in earthen vessels, that the exceeding greatness of the power may be of God, and not from ourselves; we are pressed on every side, yet not straitened; perplexed, yet not unto despair; pursued, yet not forsaken; smitten down, yet not destroyed; *always bearing about in the body the dying of Jesus, that the life also of Jesus may be manifested in our body."*

Here is how it should be done—how it *was* done in the life of Saul of Tarsus—what? This is a demonstration of the fruit of the Spirit in the area of longsuffering. If we do not suffer with Him, and for Him; we cannot live for Him or like Him. If we refuse *the dying of Jesus* then His life *cannot* and *will not* be manifested in our bodies. Please notice the specific areas where the dying of Jesus must be shared:

(1) *"Pressed on every side"*—in the battle of life foes turn up in the most unexpected places. We are fighting for our life—*but* —we have never found ourselves in a place out of which the Lord could not deliver us.

(2) *"Perplexed"* — someone well said, "put to, but not put out." This is the constant inward struggle. We pause to ask why Paul did not despair—did not give up—did not quit? *Because he knew all things were working together under God's control for His good and God's glory!*

(3) *"Pursued"*—in the midst of the battle we must sometimes run from the enemy; but we have complete confidence that he will never catch us. We will not be left in the hands of Satan.

(4) *"Smitten down"*—even when trouble has done its worst, when the persecuted man has been overtaken and struck to the ground, the blow is not fatal and he rises again" (James Denney).

The poem of Edward Sill seems much to the point just here:

> This I beheld, or dreamed it in a dream:
> There spread a cloud of dust along a plain;
> And underneath the cloud, or in it, raged
> A furious battle, and men yelled, and swords
> Shocked upon swords and shields. A prince's banner
> Wavered, then staggered backward, hemmed by foes.
> A craven hung along the battle's edge,
> And thought, "Had I a sword of keener steel—
> That blue blade that the king's son bears—but this

Blunt thing!"—he snapt and flung it from his hand,
And lowering crept away and left the field.
Then came the king's son, wounded, sore bestead,
And weaponless, and saw the broken sword,
Hilt-buried in the dry and trodden sand,
And ran and snatched it, and with battle-shout
Lifted afresh he hewed his enemy down,
And saved a great cause that heroic day.

Comment For The Week

LIKE CHRIST—In Suffering Wrong.

Andrew Murray

For this is thankworthy, if a man for conscience toward God endure grief, suffering wrongfully. For what glory is it, if, when ye be buffeted for your faults, ye shall take it patiently? But, if when ye do well, and suffer for it, ye take it patiently, this is acceptable with God. —I Pet. 2:19, 20.

It is in connection with a very every-day matter that Peter gave utterance to those weighty words concerning Christ as our Surety and Example. He is writing to servants, who at that time were mostly slaves. He teaches them "to be subject with all fear," not only to the good and gentle, but also to the froward. For, so he writes, if anyone do wrong and be punished for it, to bear it patiently is no special grace. No; but if one do well, and suffer for it, and take it patiently, this is acceptable with God; such bearing of wrong is Christlike. In bearing our sins as Surety, Christ suffered wrong from man; after His Example we must be ready to suffer wrongfully, too.

There is almost nothing harder to bear than injustice from our fellow men. It is not only the loss of pain; there is the feeling of humiliation and injustice, and the consciousness of our rights asserts itself. In what our fellow creatures do to us, it is not easy at once to recognize the will of God, who thus allows us to be tried, to see if we have truly taken Christ as our Example. Let us study that example. From him we may learn what it was that gave Him the power to bear injuries patiently.

Christ believed in suffering as the will of God. He had found it in Scripture that the servant of God should suffer. He had made Himself familiar with the thought, so that when suffering came, it did not take Him by surprise. He expected it. He knew that thus He must be perfected; and so His first thought was, not how to be delivered from it, but how to glorify God in it. This enabled Him to bear the greatest injustice quietly. He saw God's hand in it.

Christian, would you have strength to suffer wrong in the spirit in which Christ did? Accustom yourself, in everything that happens, to recognize the hand and will of God. This lesson is of more consequence than you think. Whether it be some great wrong that is done you, or some little offence that you meet in daily life, before you fix your thoughts on the person who did it, first be still, and remember, *God allows me to come into this trouble to see if I shall glorify Him in it.* This trial, be it the greatest or least, is allowed by God, and is His will concerning me. Let me first recognize and submit to *God's will* in it. Then in the rest of soul which this gives, I shall receive wisdom to know how to behave in it. With my eye turned from man to God, suffering wrong is not so hard as it seems.

Christ also believed that God would care for His rights and honour. There is an innate sense of right within us that comes from God. But he who lives in the visible, wants his honour to be vindicated at once here below. He who lives in the eternal, and as seeing the Invisible, is satisfied to leave the vindication of his rights and honour in God's hands; he knows that they are safe with Him. It was thus with the Lord Jesus. Peter writes, "He committed Himself to Him that judgeth righteously." It was a settled thing between the Father and the Son, that the Son was not to care for His own honour, but only for the Father's. The Father would care for the Son's honour. Let the Christian just follow Christ's example in this, it will give him such rest and peace. Give your right and your honour into God's keeping. Meet every offence that man commits against you with the firm trust that God will watch over and care for you. Commit it to Him who judgeth righteously.

Further, *Christ believed in the power of suffering love.* We all admit that there is no power like that of love. Through it Christ overcomes the enmity of the world. Every other victory gives only a forced submission; love alone gives the true victory over an enemy, by converting him into a friend. We all acknowledge the truth of this as a principle, but we shrink from the application. Christ believed it, and acted accordingly. He said, too, I shall have my revenge; but His revenge was that of love, bringing enemies as friends to His feet. He believed that by silence and submission, and suffering and bearing wrong, He would win the cause, because thus love would have its triumph.

And this is what He desires of us, too. In our sinful nature there is more faith in might and right than in the heavenly power of love. But he who would be like Christ must follow Him in this also, that He seeks to conquer evil with good. *The more another does him wrong, the more he feels called to love Him.* Even if it be needful for the public welfare that justice should punish the offender, he takes care that there be in it nothing of personal feeling; as far as he is concerned, he forgives and loves.

Ah, what a difference it would make in Christendom and in our churches, if Christ's example were followed! If each one who was reviled "reviled not again"; if each one who suffered "threatened not, but committed himself to Him that judgeth righteously." Fellow Christians, this is literally what the Father would have us do. Let us read and read again the words of Peter, until our soul be filled with the thought, "If, when ye do well, and suffer for it, ye take it patiently, *this is acceptable with God.*"[1]

In ordinary Christian life, where we mostly seek to fulfill our calling as redeemed ones in our own strength, such a conformity to the Lord's image is an impossibility. But in a life of full surrender, where we have given all into His hands, in the faith that He will work all in us, there the glorious expectation is awakened, that the imitation of Christ in this is indeed within our reach. For the command to suffer like Christ has come in connection with the teaching, "Christ also suffered for us, so that we, being dead to sins, might live unto righteousness."

Beloved fellow Christians, wouldst thou not love to be like Jesus, and in bearing injuries act as He Himself would have acted in thy place? Is it not a glorious prospect in everything, even in this too, to be conformed to Him? For our strength it is too high; in His strength it is possible. Only surrender thyself day to day to Him to be in all things just what He would have thee to be.

[1]See Note.

92

Believe that He lives in heaven to be the life and the strength of each one who seeks to walk in His footsteps. Yield thyself to be one with the suffering, crucified Christ, that thou mayest understand what it is to be dead to sins, and to live unto righteousness. And it will be thy joyful experience what wonderful power there is in Jesus' death, not only to atone for sin, but to break its power; and in His resurrection, to make thee live unto righteousness. Thou shalt find it *equally blessed to follow fully the footsteps of the suffering Saviour,* as it has been to trust fully and only in that suffering for atonement and redemption. Christ will be as precious as thy Example as He has been as thy Surety. Because He took thy sufferings upon Himself, thou wilt lovingly take His sufferings upon thyself. And bearing wrong will become a glorious part of the fellowship with His holy sufferings; a glorious mark of being conformed to His most holy likeness; a most blessed fruit of the true life of faith.

O Lord my God, I have heard Thy precious word: If any man endure grief, suffering wrongfully, and take it patiently, this is acceptable with God. This is indeed a sacrifice that is well-pleasing to Thee, a work that Thine own grace alone hath wrought, a fruit of the suffering of Thy beloved Son, of the example He left, and the power He gives in virtue of His having destroyed the power of sin.

O my Father, teach me and all Thy children to aim at nothing less than complete conformity to Thy dear Son in this trait of His blessed image. Lord my God, I would now, once for all, give up the keeping of my honor and my rights into Thy hands, never more again myself to take charge of them. Thou wilt care for them most perfectly. May my only care be the honour and the rights of my Lord!

I specially beseech Thee to fill me with faith in the conquering power of suffering love. Give me to apprehend fully how the suffering Lamb of God teaches us that patience and silence and suffering avail more with God, and therefore with man too, than might or right. O my Father, I must, I would walk in the footsteps of my Lord Jesus. Let Thy Holy Spirit, and the light of Thy love and presence, be my guide and strength. Amen.

NOTE

"What is it thou sayest, my son? Cease from complaining,

when thou considerest my passion, and the sufferings of my other saints. Do not say, 'To suffer this from such a one, it is more than I can or may do. He has done me great wrong, and accused me of things I never thought of. Of another I might bear it, if I thought I deserved it, but not from him!' Such thoughts are very foolish; instead of thinking of patience in suffering, or of Him by whom it will be crowned, we only are occupied with the injury done to us, and the person who has done it. No, he deserves not the name of patient *who is only willing to suffer as much as he thinks proper, and from whom he pleases.* The truly patient man asks not from whom he suffers, his superior, his equal, or his inferior; whether from a good and holy man, or one who is perverse and unworthy. But from whomsoever, how much soever, or how often soever wrong, is done him, he accepts it all as from the hand of God, and counts it gain. For with God it is impossible that anything suffered for His sake should pass without its reward.

"O Lord, let that become possible to me by Thy grace, which by nature seems impossible. Grant that the suffering wrong may by thy love be made pleasant to me. To suffer for Thy sake is most healthful to my soul."[1]

[1]From Thomas A. Kempis, *Of the Imitation of Christ,* iii 19, That the suffering of wrong is the proof of true patience.

From LIKE CHRIST by Andrew Murray, pp. 32-48.

THE FRUIT OF THE SPIRIT IS KINDNESS

To be filled with the Holy Spirit is to be filled with kindness; to be filled with Christ is to be filled with kindness; therefore, to be filled with the Spirit is to be filled with Christ.

First Day:

What is this virtue of kindness; how shall we define it? Let's call it friendliness (i.e. unselfish friendliness) then we will all know the meaning and use of the word.

Here is a poem that speaks so eloquently on this subject:

THE SIN OF OMISSION

It isn't the thing you do, Dear,
It's the thing you leave undone

Still prized by me and Mabel.
We ought to throw the stuff away
Instead of holding to it,
And I to do the thing I have tried
But somehow, I can't do it.

Kindness causes us to act like Jesus in recognizing the value and importance of our children and those of others.

Third Day:

Please read carefully these two references: Matt. 18:10 "See that ye despise not one of these little ones; for I say unto you, that in heaven their angels do always behold the face of my Father who is in heaven."

Heb. 1:14 "Are they not all ministering Spirits, sent forth to do service for the sake of them that shall inherit salvation?"

From time to time there has been some question in the mind of some as to the spiritual status of these "little ones". Note please in the above references that our Lord refers to the angels assigned to children. Wait one moment—to whom are angels sent? Heb. 1:14 states they are ministering spirits sent to serve those *"that shall inherit salvation."* Are we to conclude then that children are saved because they have angels to minister unto them? We know of no reason to assign angels to those who are living in sin (original or otherwise). We read of angels ministering to our Lord; if a child is not born with the stain of sin upon his soul (and we do not believe the doctrine of original sin) we see no reason for angels watching over them aside from the fact that they belong to God. If we believe this we will be able to be more kind to our children for it will prevent us from attributing to Satan some actions and attitudes of our children which after all are but a glaring reflection of our own shortcomings. Isn't it a sobering thought to consider God has given us a child of His attended by angels for whom we are responsible? No wonder Jesus said something about a millstone and stumbling! *We are faced squarely with the responsibility to be kind to our children.*

Fourth Day:

Luke 2:51 "And he went down with them, and came to Nazareth; and he was subject unto them: and his Mother kept

97

all these sayings in her heart."

Please think through on the thought of how very difficult it was for our Lord to constantly manifest kindness (i.e. unselfish friendliness) to His parents.

What an act of condensation it was for our Lord to live amid these humble circumstances! We are reversing the approach of the need for kindness, the real need in the hearts of Christian children.

Jesus was kind (i.e. unselfishly friendly) to His parents when He knew more than they did. It is in this area we kill more kindness than in any other. When you know you are right and others are wrong is it easy to be kind? When the issue of right and wrong is not nearly as important as maintaining the Spirit of love what do we do?

Jesus was kind (and subject to) His parents even when they were wrong in their approach and opinions. It was more important to our Lord that He obey God than to stand on His rights in the realm of opinion.

Jesus was unselfishly friendly to His parents when He knew of His future greatness. He was not restive under the care of those who were in every respect His inferiors. He was full of love and therefore full of kindness.

Fifth Day:

"Can any good thing come out of Nazareth?"

Jesus remained unselfishly friendly toward His surroundings —please consider them:

1. He worked as a carpenter, rather than resenting it (when He had formerly shared the glory of the Father's house). He spoke of the good foundations of the house of life. He had doubtless shared in laying many good foundations with His foster father Joseph. He spoke of counting the cost before you begin building a house. He had probably figured the cost of a number of very real houses for those who wanted Him to build them.

2. He lived in a little country village. What did Jesus see in and near the little town of Nazareth? Had He observed the mother hen with her brood of chicks scratching in the yard near His house? As He walked through the field on His

way home from plowing did He then see a fox scampering to his lair? —or a sparrow flitting to its nest? He was not restless at the limited humble quarters where He lived. They have become immortal by His exalted use of them. Why? He was unselfishly friendly in His attitude toward His surroundings.

Sixth Day:

"Are not two sparrows sold for a farthing?" "Neither do men put a new patch on old garments." Jesus was kind when it would have been easy to register a complaint to God. He, like many others, had to scrimp and save to furnish the bare necessities of life—have you read of:

1. The price of sparrows? How do you suppose Jesus knew the price of sparrows at the local market? Wasn't it because He often went there to spend a farthing for this humble food? Jesus created the world and the fullness thereof. He knew how sumptuously some were living, and yet neither of these considerations destroyed His unselfish friendliness toward all men and all the world in which He lived.

2. The mending of garments beyond repair? Wasn't it a crime against humanity that our Lord, the prince of glory, the fairest of ten-thousand, must worry about wearing patched garments? It was, but it did not cause Jesus to lose His kindness. What physical discomfort or difficulty would destroy my unselfish friendliness? Dear Lord, I believe, help thou my unbelief!

Seventh Day:

Matt. 9:9 "And as Jesus passed by from thence, he saw a man, called Matthew, sitting at the place of toll: and he saith unto him, Follow me. And he arose, and followed him."

There was born one day in the ancient, honorable tribe of Levi a son. He, like all other Jewish sons, especially those of the priestly class was given a careful education in Hebrew law and history. But somewhere along the way something happened; fate took a hand and matters went from bad to worse for this young son of Levi. Times were hard and the wolf looked him in the face everytime he opened the door. Something had to be done. The only job open was down in that little despised booth

—tax collecting! He took the job, but how it must have broken his spirit. Then one day he heard of this young man from Nazareth—from that day everything took a turn upward. We cannot believe that suddenly Jesus appeared at the tax booth of Matthew and called him. Jesus was in the vicinity of where Matthew worked, he could have been in the crowd to hear Jesus on several occasions. Now to the question, why was Matthew Levi, despised tax collector, willing to leave all and follow our Lord? I believe it was because of the kindness of Jesus—kindness has implicit within it a belief in the capacities of others—a faith in what God can do and will do for others. It like love (of which it is a part) hopes all things, believes all thing, never gives up, never fails. Levi, like all others, followed Jesus because He was kind.

Comment For The Week
BE KIND
By An Unknown Christian

God is love: and love is kind. Now we desire to please God. And if we ask ourselves "*how* we ought to walk and to please God" (I Thes. iv. 1), one answer is: "Be kindly-affectioned one to another" (Rom. xii. 10). "Be kind!" (Eph. iv. 32). God has no pleasure in sacrifices, ceremonies, ordinances, or worship if there is any "root of bitterness" in the heart.

The Christ-like man is the *kind* man.

Few things are more attractive than kindness. "Kind words can never die." There is a craze today for putting the Bible into modern speech. But very few have dared to alter this phrase, "Love . . . is *kind*." There is no need to do it. We all know what kindness is and we all recognize kindness when we meet it.

One writer, however, renders it: "Love . . . is always trying to do good turns to others." But *love* has no need to "try"—it is spontaneous. It cannot help being kind. Kindness is a quality, a virtue which influences the heart at all times even when it does not happen to be doing "good turns." Kindness can be detected in the face, and may be revealed by a look.

The Greek word implies "useful," "manageable," "mild," "pleasant" (as opposite to sharp, hard, and bitter). In the New

Testament, when it is used of God it is sometimes translated "gracious."

In St. Paul's inspired description of "love"—in I Cor. xiii.— he gives only two *positive* characteristics. He says, "Love is kind"; and "love rejoices in the truth." Kindness (graciousness) and truth. Now those were the two things men specially beheld in Christ Jesus. St. John says, "We beheld His glory, but in deed and truth" (I John iii. 18).

Now it is possible to be long-suffering without being kind. Many folks stand aloof and proudly bear injustice, and abuse, who have very little love in their natures. But the Christlike Christian not only suffereth long—*he is kind.* He not only patiently endures evil or opposition or unkindness, but he does good in return. He rewards evil with kindness. He does good to them that despitefully use him.

Not only in his tongue "is the law of kindness" (Prov. xxxi. 26) but that law reigns in his heart because the Royal Law is there: "Thou shalt love thy neighbor as thyself" (James ii. 8). Love not only seizes opportunities for being kind, it searches for them. We are to love "not in word and tongue, but in deed and truth" (I John iii. 18).

Have we ever meditated upon GOD'S KINDNESS? Have you noticed the prominence given by the Holy Spirit to the kindness of God? Is not this an indication of the important place that kindness should hold in our lives if we would be Christ-like?

The Scriptures tell of God's *great* kindness, His merciful kindness, His marvellous kindness, His everlasting kindness. Truly God is "wondrous kind." It is the *kind* Christian who "pleases God." He is the one that God delights to honour and delights to recognize as a son. "Love your enemies," says Christ, "and do them good, and lend, never despairing (despairing of no man); and your reward shall be great, and ye shall be sons of the Most High: for He is kind toward the unthankful and evil" (Luke vi. 35). One version gives: "For my yoke is *kind*" (Matt. xi. 30); the very same word but translated "easy." Much of our Lord's earthly life was occupied simply in doing kind things—in making people happy. Are we so occupied? St. Paul lays stress upon the power exerted by "the kindness and love of God our Saviour." He points out that while man was living in malice and envy,

101

hateful, and hating one another, this "kindness of God our Saviour and His love toward man, appeared" and conquered (Tit. iii. 3-5).

It is because of "His great love wherewith He loved us, even when we were dead through our trespasses" that He "quickened us—i.e., made us alive—together with Christ and raised us up with Him and made us sit with Him in heavenly places in Christ Jesus." But for what purpose? "That in the ages to come He might shew the exceeding riches of His grace in kindness towards us in Christ Jesus" (Eph. ii. 4-6). So all eternity will be too short to exhaust God's wondrous and everlasting kindness. How *kind* the Lord Jesus was—and is— to all! How kind to the traitor! Our blessed Lord knew that Judas would betray Him with a kiss —love debased and disfigured. Yet He did not treat him with harshness or scorn—did not even rebuke him. But He gave him the great and precious privilege of living with Him as a friend; made him treasurer of all the little earthly store He ever owned; gave him the favourite's portion—the "sop"—at the last supper and—wonder of wonders!—after the kiss of betrayal, He calls him "friend" in the last words He ever spoke to him, and by a pointed question tries to persuade Judas to realize the greatness of his sin before it is too late. Love would win back, if it were possible, even the traitor—"despairing of no man" (Luke vi. 35, R.V. marg.). No flush of anger tinges the cheek kissed by the traitor. He does not recoil from the pollution of such a touch. Divine love preached to Judas, whilst He gave Simon Peter only a look. We ought indeed to study and know—

> More about Jesus' loving deeds,
> Serving so humbly others' needs,
> Setting for us the perfect plan
> God has in mind for every man.

God's kindness is so great and abundant that a new word is needed to express it. In Scripture it is often referred to as "loving-kindness." "Let Thy loving-kindness and truth continually preserve me," cries the Psalmist (Ps. xl. 11). God is not content to forgive us, heal us, cleanse us, redeem us—He makes us kings and crowns us with crowns more precious than those wrought with corruptible things, such as silver and gold. He crowns us not only with kindness, but with lovingkindness; not only with mercies innumerable, but with *tender mercies* (Ps. ciii. 1-4). And not only are we crowned with lovingkindness and tender mercies when we crown Him Lord of our lives, but our own hearts overflow with lovingkindness, witnessing to the blessed fact that we are indeed sons of the Most High. The brightest crown we can wear is that which proclaims us kings of kindness—*lovingkindness.*

"Kind hearts are more than coronets." God's lovingkindness is the strong magnet which drew us and which binds us to Christ—and at once we too became magnetized, and by that same lovingkindness we attract others to Him.

We desire to "manifest Christ in our mortal flesh" (II Cor. iv. 10). The best way of doing this is to be *kind.* Why are we not all kinder to each other? Kindness is the one thing which floods the heart with joy, which brings happiness to the lives of others, delights the heart of our Saviour, and attracts men to the Saviour's side, whilst it gladdens and warms our own hearts. And *everyone* can be kind. The world is just hungering for kindness.

> So many gods, so many creeds,
> So many roads that wind and wind and wind,
> While yet the art of being kind
> Is all this sad world needs.

"The greatest thing we can do for our Heavenly Father," says one writer, "is to be kind to some of His children."

"While we have time, let us do good unto all men; and specially unto them that are of the household of faith" (Gal. vi. 10, Prayer Book). Again we ask: Why are we not kinder to one another? We can suggest only two reasons—for we cannot conceive of a fully-surrendered Christian being willfully unkind. The chief reason is because we do not think: the other is that we do not know.

There is an ever-increasing number of Christian workers longing to do great things for their Master. They are ever

> Seeking for some great thing to do,
> Or secret thing to know.

They often pray earnestly that God will do "a new thing." Yet the greatest thing of all is within their reach—love is kind. "You may never be clever," a Godly mother used to say to her boy, "but you can always be kind." So he set out to be kind and God has made him one of England's foremost evangelists. A missionary pioneering in South America wrote home a month or two ago, "No preaching upon this trip at all. The people could understand no language we spoke, except kindness." Thank God, *all can understand that*—love is kind.

Listen! If every believer in our land would just "be kind" to all he meets—kind in tone, in word and look, in thought and deed for one month, such a blessing would be poured out of the "windows of heaven" that there would not be room enough to receive it! You may be a window of heaven to a stricken world, by being kind.

But what is kindness? Well, do I always say kind things about people? *Unkind words can never die.* Just think of the un-Christian way *Christian* men and women talk over their friends! It is truly deplorable.

Pascal once said, "If all our friends only knew what we said about them behind their backs, we would not have four friends left us in the world." *Is this true of the way we speak?* If so, may it never be true of us again. Someone said, "Before repeating any story you should ask yourself 'Is it true? Is it necessary? Is it kind?'"

A society lady recently let slip a remark which was a revelation of the extent of this *sin*—for sin it is. We had been speaking of the way people say unkind things about each other. "Yes," she replied, "that is why no one likes to be the first to leave a drawing-room."

"But the tongue can no man tame; it is a restless evil, it is full of deadly poison" (James iii. 8). Let us then hand over the keeping of the tongue to the Lord Jesus, so that never again shall it utter an unkind word.

As God said to Moses, so He says to us: "Who hath made man's mouth? . . . Have not I the Lord? . . . I will be with thy mouth and teach thee what thou shalt say" (Ex. iv. 11, 12). We *know* it is not kind, and therefore not Christian, to pass on judgment on others and severe criticism on all their actions. If we are to live Christ-like lives, *unkind criticism must drop out of those lives.* If we love our "neighbors" we shall be as careful of their interests and feelings and reputations as of our own. Then some take a positive delight in holding up to ridicule nearly every friend they have. They pride themselves on being good mimics. Yes, and who among us has always been quite free from this practice? But is it kind? As children, we may think such people "good company." But my own beloved father's quiet comment—given after the door had closed upon a mimicker—often echoes in my memory, "My boy, beware of making friends with those who make fun of others. They will surely hold *you* up to ridicule immediately when your back is turned."

Some good folk add rudeness to their unkindness by blurting out what they think of you to your face. They are even proud (!) of the fact that they are plain people who do not hesitate to speak their minds!

But their "minds" are not ours! Candour is not a privileged right to be *rude!* Ought we not to avoid wounding our friends? We need not say all we think even when asked our "candid opinion." When we disapprove of any deed is it not kinder to ask whether some other course of action might not be wiser and better, instead of pronouncing our judgment or censure?

We can always "speak the truth in love," without being either offensive or abusive.

But love is not satisfied with refraining to give offence—it is kind. And how greatly kindness is needed by us all. The insignificant "cup of cold water" means the refreshing of a thirsty soul.

Perhaps the danger of such out-spoken unkindness is greater *in the home circle* than anywhere else. What unkind—even brutal—remarks are snapped out in the home! Some "Christian" men are "at daggers drawn" with those who prayed at the same mother's knee. How can such men love their enemies when they are not kind to their best friends?

Can we love God if we hate our brother? St. John says he is a liar who says so! (John iv. 20). Love is kind to all. There can be no exceptions. When the discourteous stare is met with on the street, or in the train, or tram, love will not glare back, but will appear unconscious of any rudeness and pray that some sweetness of expression may reward the starer with thoughts of holiness and Christ.

Kindness is, of course, a far greater thing than merely not striking back!

Kindness is love outflowing in little acts of thoughtfulness and gentleness. Kindness stops the loud-speaker when it is becoming a nuisance to our neighbors. Kindness refrains from keeping the rest of the household—or those in neighbouring flats—awake half the night by its music or revelry.

Kindness does not monopolize the conversation by a recital of its own views and doings and plannings; but graciously draws out others who have something to say, or who feel ill at ease. Kindness hastens to give honour to whom honour is due. It is careful to speak the word of praise, of cheer, of encouragement, of sympathy.

It endeavours to discern something to speak well of, and to commend. It recognizes merit and frankly says so. It is kindly to all, but kindlier to the less fortunate. It has been truly said that kindness should be lavished on the poor where it is unexpected, and on the rich who need it most.

Kindness reveals itself in a spontaneous and unsought consideration of other people's rights and an anticipation of other people's wishes and hopes.

Our Lord said, "Blessed are the peacemakers," and there is no peacemaker like lovingkindness, which takes the kindliest view of an antagonist; and never fans the flame when differences arise, and never adds fuel to the fire of hate.

But kindness must not degenerate into an amiable acquiescence in sinfulness. There are some who exalt human "love" to the forgetting of the Divine love; and nothing is so debased as a "love" that sins.

That is *not* "love" which claims the right to over-ride all laws human and Divine—as some novelists and playwrights seem to teach. Such "love" is *not* kind; and therefore is not *love*.

But we all should know what kindness is. And we all ought to know that if we are unkind we cannot be Christ-like. The badge of kindness is a smile. Kindness has a good-natured outlook on life and a good-humored desire to make the best of everything and everybody.

Kindness is the one thing we are all hungering for. And it is at the same time the easiest thing to show and the greatest thing to give.

Would you be Christ-like? Begin by being kind not only to your friends but to all—even to those who seem to be your enemies. Many *are* kind. May we all become so, by the grace of the Lord Jesus Christ.

From THE CHRISTLIKE CHRISTIAN
by An Unknown Christian, pp. 81-89

THE FRUIT OF THE SPIRIT IS GOODNESS

First Day.

"Jesus of Nazareth, how God anointed him with the Holy Spirit and with power: *who went about doing good,* and healing all that were oppressed of the devil; for God was with him." Acts 10:38

Just what is meant by the expression "doing good"—"For the Son of man came to seek and to save that which was lost." Luke 19:10. Jesus came to heal and help in the physical area of life, but all of this was subservient to His higher and primary purpose. The *good* our Lord came to do was fulfilled in providing salvation for the lost. We are not equating "goodness" with kindness or gentleness—these we have already discussed—to be *good* as our Saviour was *good* is to be possessed of the same divine purpose. Jesus might well ask the same question He asked the rich young ruler. "Why callest thou me *good?*" "There is one good even God"—am I God to you? is this the reason you call me good? If Jesus is God to us (and He is) *then we must fulfill goodness as He did—"seek and save the lost"*—we are the body of Christ are we not? Can the present body have a different purpose now than when He came the first time in the likeness of sinful flesh? It shall be our purpose during this week to explore various methods of our Lord in seeking the lost, and how we today can be like Him.

Second Day.

"(although Jesus himself baptized not, but his disciples), he left Judea, and departed again into Galilee. And he must needs pass through Samaria. So he cometh to a city of Samaria called Sychar, near to the parcel of ground that Jacob gave to his son Joseph: and Jacob's well was there. Jesus therefore, being wearied with his journey, sat thus by the well. It was about the sixth hour. There cometh a woman of Samaria to draw water: Jesus saith unto her, Give me to drink. For his disciples were gone away into the city to buy food. The Samaritan woman therefore saith unto him, How is it that thou, being a Jew, asketh drink of me, who am a Samaritan woman? (For Jews have no dealings with Samaritans.) Jesus answered and said unto her, If thou knewest the gift of God, and who it is that saith to thee, Give me to drink; thou wouldest have asked of him, and he would have given thee living water. The woman saith unto him, Sir, thou hast nothing to draw with, and the well is deep: whence then hast thou that living water? Art thou greater than our father Jacob, who gave us the well, and drank thereof himself, and his sons, and his cattle? Jesus answered and said unto her, Every one that drinketh of this water shall thirst again: but whosoever drinketh of the water that I shall give him shall never thirst; but the water that I shall give him shall become in him a well of water springing up into eternal life. The woman saith unto him, Sir, give me this water, that I thirst not, neither come all the way hither to draw. Jesus saith unto her, God, call thy husband and come hither. The woman answered and said unto him, I have no husband. Jesus saith unto her, Thou saidst well, I have no husband: for thou hast had five husbands; and he whom thou now hast is not thy husband: this hast thou said truly. The woman saith unto him, Sir, I perceive that thou art a prophet. Our fathers worshipped in this mountain; and ye say, that in Jerusalem is the place where men ought to worship. Jesus saith unto her, Woman, believe me, the hour cometh, when neither in this mountain, nor in Jerusalem, shall ye worship the Father. Ye worship that which ye know not: we worship that which we know; for salvation is from the Jews. But the hour cometh, and now is, when the true worshippers shall worship the Father in spirit and truth: for such doth the Father seek to be his worshippers. God is a Spirit: and they that worship him must worship in spirit and truth. The woman saith unto him, I know that Messiah cometh (he that is called Christ): when he is come, he will declare unto us all things. Jesus saith unto her, I that speak unto thee am He." John 4: 2-26.

We are indebted to C. J. Sharp in his book *Personal Evangelism* for the outline in this section.

How Can I Have the Fruit of the Spirit?

To Jesus the Samaritan woman presented an opportunity for heavenly work. How many opportunities have we met and passed by as of too difficult, or an "impossible case"? Please mark carefully the example of our Lord in doing the "good" of God—seeking and saving the lost:

(1) He was traveling, yet He won a soul on the way. We think immediately of Philip and the Ethiopian eunuch who would match this example. How many times have we sat down alongside some poor lost soul and failed to "ask them for a drink of water" or hesitated to ask them "if they understood the scripture?" There is not always an easy way to introduce the subject of salvation, but if we have the compassion of our Lord we will make one.

(2) It was high noon and luncheon time, yet He thought first of the bread of life for a perishing soul. He said He was as interested in the eternal welfare of this woman as the average person would be in eating. Jesus relished His work of soul-winning like a hungry man relishes food. Oh, for the constraint of hungering for souls—most of all if we could pray with real meaning and feeling "give me souls or I die"? Look at the obvious eagerness and positive satisfaction with which a very hungry man eats food—look again—this was the same attitude our Lord displayed in His speaking to the Samaritan woman of her relationship to God.

(3) He was tired and hungry, yet He did not allow that fact to cause Him to put off the opportunity. Are we going to allow the demands of our bodies to dictate the choices of our spirits? Are we body-slaves or spirit-slaves?— which is dominant in our choices? Why are we so irrational when we are tired?—How is it that we act so much more like beasts than men when we are full of fatigue? You have the answer—we know it is because we yield our spirits to the demands of the body—we cooperate in the cravings of the flesh for rest (or food). When rest or food is delayed we are full of resentment; we resist such delay; we begrudgingly continue in anything that prolongs such a delay—but why? *Because the*

demands of the body are our dominant point of interest.
It was not so with our Lord. When will we sign our
Saviour's emancipation proclamation—"Let a man deny
himself"?

Third Day.

(4) The opportunity seemed small, only one, and that one
a strange woman. I wonder, where was the pessimism
that usually accompanies contact with harlots and drunk-
ards? We all know that there surely is very little or anything one can do with a prostitute or a drunkard—
evidently Jesus didn't know this! What seemed impossible on surface appearance offered a grand possibility
to God. Wouldn't it have been much more reasonable to
eat, and then go into Samaria and gather a crowd and
speak to several hundred than to only one?—and what
a one! Our Lord knew the hundreds in the town would
listen with more understanding—and with a greater
desire to believe what this woman had to say once she
had found for herself the Saviour of the world.

If we accept our Lord's estimate of one soul we will
believe that one soul won is of more value than all the
wealth of all the world—but—who knows the eternal
wealth to others that one soul might have—?

(5) The one to be won was a despised woman of a despised
people. I wonder—what does a negro prostitute look
like? Have you ever seen one? Perhaps some of you
have—most of us are not looking for them. There are
however over five million negroes in our country and
many, many of them are the victims or slaves of the lust
of the flesh. What shall be our attitude toward the prostitutes in this group? Someone immediately objects, that
we cannot thus classify and discuss our responsibility to
the whole class of negro prostitutes—why not? If we are
not concerned about all of them, how will we discover
the one who could be saved, and who could save others?
We can become very idealistically and sentimentally concerned for the Samaritan woman as long as she does not
suddenly turn into a negro prostitute. How much real
good do we want to do?—perhaps we should stay out of

our Samaria—it is too embarrassing. On the other hand it might be the Holy Spirit bearing witness to our conscience (Rom. 9: 1,2).

Fourth Day.

(6) Excuses were abundant, but none of them stopped Him. There are always so very many good reasons why this person or that one would not listen or if they did why it would do no good. Many excuses can be ignored— reasons for refusal can be answered—provided we have the same concern to win the lost our Lord had when He opened the conversation with the Samaritan woman.

So many times excuses are but another way of asking for help. The woman of our text was deeply discouraged —she wanted help, but was not at all sure there was anyone who could help her. As we have said elsewhere— objections to Jesus were but signal flags of distress. Jesus proceeded to answer the need.

(7) His method of approach was tactful and not offensive. So much of our understanding of fact is mis-understanding. Tact is simply the ability to keep the mind and heart of the listener open for communication. There is not one way to be tactful, there are hundreds. It is almost impossible to accept the recommendations of another if we resent them. Jesus surely did not side-step the sin in the life of this woman—but in speaking of her sin He kept her mind and heart open or receptive—she never once felt our Lord had lost interest in her as an individual— she believed from first to last—"here is a man full of compassion for me and my deepest need."

Fifth Day.

(8) He did not turn away because the woman did not at first (seem) to appreciate His meaning and purpose. We come not to help the well but the sick. Are we prompted in our service to serve because we are appreciated—or because we see and feel a need that must be met? Please remember the prophets and the response to their messages. We must love people because God loves them and we love God. The more we love God the more it is possible to share His love (many, many times unre-

quited) with the lost world. Jesus said, "If you knew . . ."
—what a poignant word. But He was not satisfied to
sink down in sentimentalism and self-righteousness as if
to say "If you only what I know—or who I am—". He
pressed the case until it was possible for her to know.

(9) He did not allow her to turn from His point. Why are
folk so eager to change the subject?

For the same reason as that which prompted this woman.
Satan is back of this attempt of evasion. She did not
know which to say in answer to Jesus' searching request
—"Go, call thy husband"—The best she could offer was
the transparently weak attempt to cover her sin—"I have
no husband". How often this has happened in the home
of some needy person. When the finger of God touches
the sore spot the subject is changed! Why? No one
likes to face his sin. It is easier to hide behind some
familiar moot question. There really is no answer but
the discussion will relieve the pressure. Although Jesus
did not ignore her question about the place to worship
neither did He lose sight of His point. He must speak
to her of the heart need. He must reach her in the deepest
recesses of her subconscious being. He never lost sight of
His objective. This we *must* learn if we are to win souls.

Sixth Day.

(10) He unerringly drove home the truth about both sin and
God. Until both of these subjects become real to the
prospect we had just as well forget about winning them
to the salvation in Christ Jesus. There must be an understanding of the personal moral responsibility of every
man to God. The woman at the well was Jewish. This
meant she was conscious of God and His law as well as
her personal responsibility to it. There are so very many
people in our day and country (to say nothing of other
countries) who have no awareness of their personal responsibility to a personal God! Until the Bible is accepted as the word of God—we mean God speaking to
us in the words of the book called the Holy Bible—we
have no common ground upon which to stand in our
discussion of sin and God. More than the above truth

is the fact: until the Bible speaks personally to us—until it is God's will for your life and mine, we have only a mental acquiescence to a cold fact. We must feel it is God who speaks out of the pages and from the words of this book Jesus made the woman keenly, painfully, personally, aware of sin. What is sin? "Sin is the transgression of God's law." (I John 3:4). The law she had violated was "Thou shalt not commit adultery." (Ex. 20:14; Deut. 5:18). Until the prospect is made to relate himself to God's law in a personal manner you have lost in your attempt to win. "He whom thou now hast is not thy husband." This statement of our Lord related law to life. It is well enough to believe that "all have sinned" —that no one has escaped the transgression of one or more of God's laws, but it is another matter to cause the prospect to awaken to his personal violation of God's law and feel in his conscience his personal guilt. Fastened to sinning is the consequence. We cannot miss the mark and yet receive a prize. We cannot violate God's law and miss the penalty. God has but *one penalty* for sin—"The wages of sin is death." (Rom. 6:23). He has but one reason for the second death and that is sin. (Rev. 21:1-8). When your prospect is faced squarely with his sin against God and his consequent lost condition he is in the same position into which Jesus led the woman at the well. You *must unerringly drive home the truth of both sin and God.*

Seventh Day.

(11) He convinced, convicted and won the woman, so that she became, in turn, one to bring many others to him. The woman was not only convinced of her sin and her need but of the grand deliverance offered by the Messiah —the unlimited power of the Messiah was known and believed by all the children of Israel. This is surely not the situation with so very many all about us. When once we have brought conviction of sin (the Holy Spirit's work through the Word) we must yet remember that a convicted sinner without a Saviour is in the worst possible state. We must be careful to hold ever before him

113

the suffering Saviour who is well able to save unto the uttermost all those who come to Him. Concurrent with a view of the sinfulness of sin must be the worthiness of the Saviour from sin. Jesus did not come as some policeman to find us in our sin and accuse us of our guilt, but He came as a Saviour to find us in our sins and to save us *from* them.

Please notice the reaction of the woman her salvation. *She herself became a "saviour".* Not, of course, in the same sense as our Lord, but she was directly responsible for the salvation of a multitude from her hometown of Sycar. If our salvation does not issue forth in gratitude to others in the same need in which we were found there is something deadly defective about it. Oh, that the joy, wonder and deep appreciation possessed by the woman of Jacob's well might be in those we win to the same Saviour. Didn't Jesus say the water He would give would become an artesian well of refreshment? Didn't our Lord say ". . .whosoever drinketh of the water that I shall give him shall never thirst." Why are we then surprised at the woman's reactions?

(12) He used the incident further to prepare His disciples that they might be equipped to be winners of souls.

Every personal evangelist should be a teacher of others in this glorious work. Every experience of winning one should teach us principles to be used in winning many more. Please read verses 27 through 38 of the fourth chapter of John. There are yet many disciples who will marvel that we engage strange sinners in conversation about their need of living water. Even if we do not hear the criticism firsthand it will be given by the very ones who ought to be engaged in the very work they criticize. Settle it in your mind: when those who have a conscience about witnessing observe someone doing what they are not doing (and know they should) the very first reaction is to find fault with the method and so to rationalize away their total lack in either method or means. Jesus taught His concern for souls by example. There are three areas where man speaks of his concern very plainly:

(1) sex, (2) food, (3) money. When you prefer soul-winning to any one of these subjects you have become like your example. The sex, food and money of Jesus was His Father's will of seeking and saving the lost! The disciples were prepared to lift up their eyes to the white harvest field only after Jesus opened their eyes to the need and opportunity by His example. How many other eyes could be opened to harvest of eternal spirits if we would only let Jesus open our eyes? What does it mean to "gather fruit unto life eternal?" Can we accept the implications of this statement? There is a work eternal in value. There is a life after this one. We can save souls from eternal death to eternal life. We can gather for the eternal garner. Tell me my soul—"believest thou this"?

COMMENT FOR THE WEEK

There are so very many ways to seek and save the lost. In the use of any and every method we want to have "the mind of Christ". God expects every Christian to be a soulwinner. The example of the church in the New Testament indicates that God's expectations can be fulfilled. It can be today. There is not one way to win the lost; there are *many!*

ELEVEN WAYS TO SEEK AND SAVE THE LOST

1. *Use gospel tracts*—Read this wonderful statement concerning the power of a tract, written by one who built a business publishing tracts:

"My message is always clear and brief. I can speak any language. I am never rushed, nor is any distance too great for me to travel to reach one soul. Unlike many missionaries, I need no regular support, nor must I pay room and board when staying in a foreign country. No special permission is required from the government when I enter or leave a country.

I remember one day in France when I began to witness to a man who didn't want to hear about Christ. He was so angry that he finally pushed me into the street and walked on me. There I lay in the cold wet street unable to get up. But I am never sick.

Finally a kind-hearted woman came along and helped me up. I traveled with her to her home that night to tell her son about

Christ and His power to save. I invited him to a gospel service which he attended and before long he was converted to Christ.

One day I was riding in a car with some Christian friends through a small village. One of my friends pushed me out the window. Quickly a man came over and lifted me up. Now some missionaries would have to introduce themselves to a stranger before they witnessed of Christ, but I started right away to tell this kind man of Jesus' love and death on the cross for him. He was to busy to stand and talk, so I traveled along the street with him. He wanted to hear more.

I can't carry Bibles with me on my travels, but this time I gave the man an address to which he could write and get a New Testament. He has his Testament now and is reading it regularly.

Often my travels take me to beds of the sick and dying, but I fear no disease; I can work myself into broken homes, hospitals, prisons, and many of my brothers have gone behind the iron curtain of Russia and the bamboo curtain of Asia.

We can preach the gospel everywhere and the police cannot kill us. For, you see, our life is not physical life. We are only made of paper and ink and yet we bring strength to weak bodies, hope to the despairing and faith to the fearful. Our life is the power of God behind the words printed on our pages.

Perhaps you have friends or loved ones who are unconverted. They may live too far away for you to visit them and tell them of Christ. Or they might not listen to your words of witness.

I will be glad to come to your house and you may introduce me to your friends. Some of them may find Christ as their personal Saviour from sin through reading my pages.

Pray that God will bless my missionary work and will lead me to souls who are seeking eternal life."

From "I AM A SILENT MESSENGER"
By Good News Publishers

Set up and Maintain a tract station.

Attractive tract racks and available for a reasonable price. Here is where you can buy them: *Herald Press Tracts,* Scottdale, Pennsylvania

Here are some places to locate them:

(1) In a bus station

(2) In an airport
(3) In a train depot
(4) In a service station
(5) In a restaurant
(6) In a laundramat
(7) In a rest-home
(8) In a hospital
(9) In a garage
(10) In a grocery-store
(11) In a church-house
(12) In a drug store

There are doubtless a dozen more places you could think of where the gospel can be made available to those who hurry down the broad way that leads to destruction.

When you do set-up a literature distribution center (a tract rack) please, please be responsible for keeping it stocked. There is little use in setting up a tract station if you are not going to keep tracts in it. Check at least once a week or oftener to insure it is doing its job. Stamp or print on each tract a name and address and/or phone number to which the interested can refer.

What would it mean to the lost world if every Christian would covenant with our Lord that they would either give or send one tract per day for the next 30 days? Should we do less? Do we care? Can we ignore this obvious grand opportunity of reaching the lost?

There are many, many good tracts available from the two following addresses:

(1) College Press, Box 1132, Joplin, Missouri 64802
(2) Christian Publishing Co., 2652 Brenner Dr., Dallas, Texas 75220

2. *Visit Jesus in your local hospital!*

"Lord, when saw we thee sick . . . and came unto thee? And the King shall answer and say unto them (you), Inasmuch as ye did it unto one of these my brethren; even these least, ye did it unto me." (Matt. 25: 39,40)

Folk are so very, very lonely—in a hospital or rest-home. They pause long enough to feel it. Your coming is so very welcome to so very many. In contrast to house-to-house calling, you are usually eagerly sought in your hospital calls. Perhaps this is why more preachers make hospital calls than any other type. But such calls must not—need not be limited to the preacher. Every Christian has the high privilege of visiting our Lord in the person of "one of the least of these". Will you do it? When you do, here are a few things to remember in your hospital calling: (From GUIDE LINES TO HOSPITAL VISITATION by Archie L. Miller)

"Learn visiting hours ahead of time. Have local hospital visitor's rules explained before visiting. Observe all hospital rules and regulations. If you are sick, stay away. Have the information clerk direct you to the one you are visiting, thus avoiding straying into forbidden area. If the patient's door is closed, have nurse check before entering. It's a good idea to stop at the nurse's desk and ask for permission to visit; last minute requirements may necessitate your waiting or coming back later. Acknowledge other patients present.

The patient's bedside is his living room and you are his guest. Approach the patient with genuine love and concern. If the patient is sleeping, don't waken him; rest is what he needs rather than company. Stand where the patient can easily see you. Don't position yourself so you have a glare or strong light behind your head. Sit down if he invites you to do so but don't sit on the patient's bed. Don't kick, hit or jar the bed for this can be very painful. Watch for equipment, bottles, tubes, or pans under, around or attached to bed — and do not disturb them. Keep your visit short — about 15 minutes is right. Watch your own nervous habits. Make sure the patient knows who you are. Be yourself as the patient knows you. Keep number of visitors down; two visitors at a time is a good rule. Remember, patients tire easily. Come back later if he has had several visitors prior to your arrival. Don't whisper to others in patient's audio/visual range. Talk in normal conversational tones. Be a good listener and hear him out — but don't make him entertain you. Don't play doctor or psychiatrist and try to diagnose. Don't climb into bed with the patient and share your illnesses. If patients desire to tell of their ailments, listen, but don't dwell on it. Be calm and relaxed but don't overdo it. Don't appear shocked at the strange smells or sights. Let the patient take the initiative in offering you a chair or shaking hands. Pray for the patient but with meaning and briefly. Check with the nurse before giving anything to the patient; he many not be allowed water and candy may be taboo. Don't argue with the patient; an argument may cause a set-back — and — his decisions will perhaps be no healthier than he is when he made them. It may be against hospital's regulations to distribute tracts or religious literature from bed to bed but this will not hinder you from personal distribution. Under no circumstances administer medication to the patient."

3. *Call in a rest-home.*

Couldn't you set-up a regular calling program for the rest-homes or convalescent homes in your community? What would a word of encouragement—an appropriate scripture passage—a sincere well worded prayer mean to these folk? If you have ever had the privilege of such calling, you know you are ashamed that you have not been there sooner, and more often. The caller receives a double benefit from such calls:

(1) He becomes aware of the gratitude he should have for good health.

(2) He finds great satisfaction in an actual, tangible, personal service for Christ.

When will you start? Jesus is waiting and looking for you from that hospital bed or rest-home wheel-chair — will you come?

4. *Take A Religious Census*—and follow-up with other forms of service.

A religious survey should be made of every community every six months. This is especially true of a large town or city. People are moving. A very high percentage of the people who now live in your neighborhood will not be living there six months from now. (Of course, there are exceptions in towns of 100 or 200 residents, but we are speaking of communities over a thousand in population.) Talk to a leader of the Jehovah Witness or the Latter Day Saints, or the Seventh Day Adventists and ask them how often they canvass a community in promoting their cause. Once every six months is a conclusion from conversations with the above named persons. Are we going to do less for New Testament Christianity?

When you do take a census, go two-by-two. Let one person ask the questions and the other one write down the answers. Here is a sample card of the many available:

CENSUS CARD

Family Name				Address			Phone Number					
Not Home ( )	Vacant ( )			Construction ( )		Refused ( )		Minister To Call ( )				
Names of Occupants	**Birth**				**Church Affiliation of Family**			**Atten**		**Pros**		
	Age	Month	Day	Year	Name of Church	Name of Bible School	Church Preference	Regular	Occas. Unable	Bible Sc	Ch Mem	Worker
Husband												
Wife												
Child												
Child												
Child												
Child												
Parents Occupation	Husband			Wife		Sun. Work Hus ( ) Wf ( )		Date of Call				

Census Taker's Remarks:

Sweany Print, Fair Play, Mo.

There are a number of places where such cards can be purchased. Here are two of them:

(1) Christian Publishing Co., 2652 Brenner Dr., Dallas, Texas 75220

(2) Ozark Bible College Bookstore, 1111 N. Main, Joplin, Missouri 64801

5. *Follow up the census with direct mail advertising for Christ's Church.*

What is Direct Mail for Christ? There is a filmstrip and record available to tell you all about it. This is produced by the non-instrument Church of Christ of Bedford, Texas. Here is a quotation from their paper: *Reporter of* DIRECT MAIL EVANGELISM.

This "DIRECT MAIL FOR CHRIST" film and record set tells the story in a way that is suitable for showing to your business meeting, Wednesday or Sunday evening worship service, or to area gatherings or lectureships. When it was first shown at the breakfast before a group of preachers and others (mostly from the northern USA and Canada), two of those present volunteered to pay for the transposing of the slides into filmstrip form, and for placing a narration on a 12 inch LP record.

This set has been shown before hundreds of congregations, perhaps thousands. It informs of the power of the written word from the time of the first century until the present age, and acquaints the viewer with the services of the government mail. Direct mail has been proven and found to be most effective not only by commercial advertising firms (over 2,500,000,000 dollars in the USA last year), but also in conveying the message of the gospel.

The set is available from the Brown Trail Church of Christ, 1801 Brown Trail, Bedford, Texas, for a 10 day loan without charge or for $5 if purchased.

The elders of the Brown Trail church wish to express their sincere gratitude to all for the encouraging letters and generous support in this venture of faith. They at the same time want to plead for the patience of all concerned while the first issues are being published. Many Christians are working literally night and day in getting the first issue in the mail . . . and this is not difficult to understand in view of the fact that there are over one million papers involved.

Your prayers are sorely needed as we strive together with God in publishing the truth "throughout the whole region"! Write to: 1801 Brown Trail, Bedford, Texas for further information.

6. *Write Letters Abroad For Christ.*

Please let me explain. In many places on this earth, ministers and missionaries have new Christians that need Christian nurture. This is most especially true on the foreign field. Many of the converts in another country can read and write English—(many times they are happy for the opportunity to practice their English) —such persons need help. You, perhaps, can give them that help through correspondence. Write to a missionary of your acquaintance and ask him about it. Write to Mission Services of Box 968, Joliet, Illinois for a complete list of the more than 800 missionaries.

Someone-somewhere is waiting for your letter — will you write it?

7. *Use Billboards For Christ.*

Have you ever seen a thirty-foot sign on the highway advertising that Christ died for our sins? Perhaps you have—such signs are available at the following address: The Bible Crusaders, P.O. Box 777, Seattle, Washington - 98111. From another address you can obtain signs especially designed to assist in promoting the Lord's Church. We refer to The Outdoor Parson - Peru, Indiana. Please contact the nearest outdoor advertising agency and ask what arrangements can be made to place these signs. A strip or a banner carrying the name and address of the local church should be produced to include on the bottom of each sign, so as to personalize the message. Renting a billboard for Christ would be a grand class project. Are we really interested in allowing the Holy Spirit to prompt and probe our conscience in seeking and saving the lost? Here is a way to speak to thousands. Who will be the first to do it?

8. *Dial a Devotion.*

The telephone company has a service you can use for Christ. A recording device is used which makes it possible to repeat to the listener a one, two, or three minute message every time they dial a certain number. Business firms use this method to advertise their products—we can use it to reach hearts for Christ. Prepare several one or two minute scripts, (how many words do you use in a minute in reading audibly?) Go down to your telephone office and transcribe these messages. Print cards giving the phone number folk can call when they feel in need of a spiritual lift. Use the books, OUT OF MY TREASURE, VOL. I & II, published in 1964 - 1965 by College Press. These two columns are full of material you can use for Dial a Devotion. Place a one inch ad in the newspaper — in the personal column — stating the opportunity for comfort and spiritual help by dialing a certain number. This avenue of service is not confined to just the preacher. There are many elders, deacons, teachers, or just *you* who could speak to the needs of many in a most meaningful manner. Visit your phone company and find the costs and procedures involved.

9. *Teach In the Home Through Film Strips and Records.*

This is best when done by appointment. The whole procedure of home teaching is so well described and visualized on color film strips by Jule Miller, that the best I can do is to recommend you rent for 25¢, the set of film strips from the Ozark Bible College Library (1111 North Maint St., Joplin, Missouri). You can buy these film strips with instructions on how to use them from *Gospel Services, Inc.,* 1409 Rosalie, Houston, Texas, 77004.

10. *Teach In the Home With Gospel Sales Manuals.*

I know of no better way to describe this procedure of teaching the gospel in the home. All of us are acquainted with the salesman and his manual. Why not visualize the message of Christ in the same way insurance or encyclopedias are visualized? This has been done! Such visualized teaching manuals with instructions on how best to use them are available from the *College Press.* Here are some of them: MORE THAN CONQUERORS HERE'S HOW (also included instruction manual on how to use this book); YOU AND ME AND GOD (also included instruction manual on how to use this book); YOUR RELIGION (also included instruction manual on how to use this book); THE LORD'S CHURCH, THE LORD'S GIFT, THE LORD'S SUPPER (also included instruction manual on how to use this book); TEN TIMELY TRUTHS (instruction manual included).

After using one or more of these grand teaching aids it will occur to you that you could make a better one. We want to encourage you to do so! Send us a copy when you do — we would like to offer it to thousands of other potential soulwinners.

11. *Use a correspondence course to reach the lost.*

Place an ad in your local newspaper or in a widely read magazine stating the opportunity of obtaining a free Bible Study course. Use the course as a follow up for a radio program. You can be the teacher of those who have a real interest in the Bible. They have such an interest or they would never have inquired in answer to your advertisement. Use a course with as few lessons as possible —both because it will cos; you less and because the new student will have a sense of accom₁'ishment. Send the student the first lesson with the exam. Enclose an envelope with your address, so he can mail the examination to you. Please, please, keep a personal contact going between you and the correspondent student. It is so easy to lose interest if letters are not frequent. Here are a list of several correspondence courses and where you can obtain them:

Christian Publishing Co. Inc., 2652 Brenner Drive, Dallas, Texas 75220

THE FRUIT OF THE SPIRIT IS FAITHFULNESS

First Day.

Matt. 7:21-25: "Not every one that saith unto me, Lord, Lord, shall enter into the kingdom of heaven; but he that doeth the will of my Father who is in heaven. Many will say to me in that day, Lord, Lord, did we not prophesy by thy name, and by thy name do many mighty works? And then will I profess unto them, I never knew you: depart from me, ye that work iniquity. Every one therefore that heareth these words of mine, and doeth them, shall be likened unto a wise man, who built his house upon the rock: and the rain descended, and the floods came, and the winds blew, and beat upon that house; and it fell not: for it was founded upon the rock."

All will agree our Lord was the essence of faithfulness; the more we are like Him the closer we are to being filled with faithfulness; we believe the Holy Spirit will enable us to produce this fruit in our character.

Perhaps a definition of the term would not be out of place; somehow this word is clouded in the understanding of some folk —do we know more of the meaning of the term "patience" or "steadfastness"? We are discussing the patience or steadfastness of the Spirit.

For today and tomorrow and the next day, we want to consider some false sources of steadfastness, perhaps we should say—some half-truths as to the source of faithfulness—what are the underlying motivations for patience?

Someone could say, "If a man will walk and talk with Jesus for awhile, he will become steadfast or faithful." On the surface this sounds fine, but we all know someone who walked and talked with our Lord for more than three years and yet denied Him—not once—but three times. We can associate with a person for years and yet really never know him. Even when that person is Jesus, He may never have made penetration into the inner consciousness of the follower. Peter found that walking and talking with Jesus was not enough—companionship is one thing—commitment is another. Peter denied Christ *after* he had called Him

124

Lord! It is only when our confession is a commitment that it relates to faithfulness.

Second Day.

Matt. 12:47-50: "And one said unto him, Behold, thy mother and thy brethren stand without, seeking to speak to thee. But he answered and said unto him that told him, Who is my mother? and who are my brethren? And he stretched forth his hand towards his disciples, and said, Behold, my mother and my brethren! For whosoever shall do the will of my Father who is in heaven, he is my brother, and sister, and mother."

Someone else said, "Our problem is one of education—if we just knew what to say and when to say it we would grow and go for God." Once again this is only a half-truth. We do have need for education, but this is no answer to the problem of backsliding. Have you heard of Jonah the preacher? He was well educated in the will of God, but he was anything but faithful to God. Jonah not only knew the will of God but he knew just where and when God wanted it to be expressed.

Read again the text for today—knowledge is no substitute for surrender. What was it that kept Jonah from accepting the will of God for him? Was it his family, his job?; it surely was some other interest that dominated his will in the place of God. Jesus is here teaching us that we must let God's will become so dominant that all other interests are sublimated to it, and become in a very real sense subordinate to it.

Third Day.

John 4:31-34: "In the meanwhile the disciples prayed him, saying, Rabbi, eat. But he said unto them, I have meat to eat that ye know not. The disciples therefore said one to another, Hath any man brought him aught to eat? Jesus saith unto them, My meat is to do the will of him that sent me, and to accomplish his work."

The third half-truth is sometimes stated in these words: "I have been running with the wrong crowd—what I need is Christian friends—if I could associate with them I know I could overcome my lack of interest and would become steadfast." Have you ever heard of the disciple who had the very finest of Christian com-

panions?—companions like Luke, Paul, Barnabas, Peter, Timothy —and yet he loved this present world and became an apostate— surely you know of Demas. He knew of Jesus—he knew the will of God for his life—he had Christian friends—and *all of these are a wonderful help when we are hungry to do God's will and accomplish His work in our lives!* Our Lord is saying to us in the text for today—your desire to do God's will in your life should be as dominant as your desire for food—indeed should supercede it. We anticipate with real eagerness a well prepared meal. Why? —because we are hungry. Where is our appetite for God's will? We are very faithful to the dinner table—because of our desire. There is a wonderful satisfaction in doing God's will—we will never know this until we come to His table and dine.
Fourth Day.

Matt. 6:9, 10: "After this manner therefore pray ye: Our Father who are in heaven, Hallowed be thy name. Thy kingdom come. Thy will be done as in heaven, so on earth."

What does the mis-named "Lord's Prayer" have to do with faithfulness? Look at the opening request of this beautiful prayer. "Hallowed be thy name." *Here is the source of faithfulness— absolute devotion to God.* This is expressed in a holy reverence for Him in every area of life. The name of God stands for God Himself. Take a consciousness of God into your classroom, your work-shop, your kitchen. Where we can say from the depth of our being, "all life is sacred—made sacred by God's presence and approval"; then we will out of this awareness be faithful. This is spontaneous steadfastness. There is nothing forced or coerced in this expression of service; it arises naturally out of gratitude, respect, love for God. This is the tap-root of "patience in well doing"—have you seen a great tree toppled over by a storm? The roots were exposed; you will look a long time before you see a fallen giant with a great tap-root—such trees are not blown over by the wind! The reverence (holy awe) of the Lord is the beginning and end of our steadfast service.

Fifth Day.

Matt. 5:13-16: "Ye are the salt of the earth: but if the salt have lost its savor, wherewith shall it be salted? it is thence forth good for nothing, but to be cast out and trodden under foot of men. Ye are the light of the world. A city set on a hill cannot be hid. Neither do men light a lamp and put it under a bushel, but on the stand; and it shineth unto all that are in the house. Even so let your light shine before men; that they may see your good works, and glorify your Father who is in heaven."

We come now to an essential supporting root of the great taproot—*a constant awareness that we represent a far greater cause than ourselves.* If we must count only on our contribution to the Lord's work, we could easily become very discouraged—for oft times all our efforts are very feeble. But when we remember we are only a part (sometimes a very small part) of a much grander cause than ourselves, we take courage to let our light shine (however small it may be). The words of the poet are much to the point.

"I am only one, but I am one. I can't do everything, but
I can do something. And what I can do, that I ought to do.
And what I ought to do, by the Grace of God I shall do."
—Edward Everett Hale.

We are citizens of the eternal kingdom; we are sharing in the glory of the King of Kings and Lord of Lords; we are soldiers in the army that has never lost a battle; we serve under a commander who holds all authority, in heaven, as well as on earth. These considerations give us a sense of security—an awareness that our labors together are not at all vain—indeed together we make up an invincible force. Please remember the whole body, the whole army, the whole kingdom.

Sixth Day.

Matt. 6:24; 12:30: Faithfulness comes from a single source—devotion to a cause or a person—we have both; but *our devotion must also be single*—when our loyalty is divided we destroy the strength of our faithfulness. May we ask our Father to strengthen us by His Spirit in the inward man that we might be like His son —consider Him:

(1) When He was twelve years old He said: "Know ye not I *must* be about my Father's business" (Luke 2:49).

127

(2) At the beginning of His ministry He said: *"Suffer it now* for thus it becometh us to fulfill all righteousness" (Matt. 3:15).

(3) In the wilderness with Satan He said: *"It is written"* (Matt. 4:4). His devotion was fixed—His eye was single.

(4) With the man born blind He said, "We *must* work the works of Him that sent me while it is yet day . . ." (John 9:4).

(5) In the midst of His ministry at Capernaum while he taught and healed unto the setting of the sun. In the morning a great crowd came around Him and urged Him to stay with them. What did He say? "I *must* preach the good tidings of the kingdom of God in other cities also, . . . for *therefore* was I sent" (Luke 4:43).

Seventh Day.

Faithfulness costs something—"neither will I offer burnt offerings unto the Lord my God of that which doth cost me nothing" (II Sam. 24:24). If it costs nothing it is worth nothing—either to the user or the observer. Are we willing to pay the price of faithfulness?—Our Lord was willing—When will we cease calling Him Lord when we are unwilling to pay the price?

Jesus drank many lesser cups of the Father's will before Gethsemane. Every day, in so many situations, we are faced with the choice of whether we shall drink the cup.

Is it the Father's will for you to study personally, devotionally, systematically His wonderful word? Will you this day drink this cup? Is it the Father's will for you to list for prayer the names and needs of lost men and women—and pray consistently for them?—will you this day drink this cup?

Is it the Father's will for you to set up a definite daily calling program? There are so many who could be helped by your visit—will you this day drink this cup?

There is but little purpose in thinking of some momentous Gethsemane in our lives if we refuse on a lesser level to do His will. Faithfulness means keeping faith with Him who kept faith with and for us.

Comment For The Week

THE BELIEVER'S PART IN BECOMING SPIRITUAL: FAITH

By Ruth Paxson

Some here may say "As far as I know I have yielded my life wholly to Christ, yet I still seem to be living on the plane of the carnal Christian. Is it possible to be yielded and yet not filled with the Holy Spirit?" Yes, the emptied life waits for faith to claim the fullness.

Surrender says, "Lord, I am not my own. I present my body a living sacrifice." Faith says, "Christ liveth in me." Surrender says, "Lord, what wilt Thou have me to do?" Faith says, "I can do all things through Christ which strengtheneth me." Surrender crowns Christ Lord. Faith appropriates Christ as Life. Stephen was "full of faith and of the Holy Spirit."

Faith is the Complement of Grace

Did you ever see a perfect rainbow? Usually one end is perfect and the other seems to go off into nothing. Looking out over the ocean I once saw distinctly both ends of a rainbow coming up out of the water, as it were, and forming an unbroken arch. Through this beautiful symbol the Holy Spirit interpreted to me the relationship faith has to grace in salvation as revealed in Ephesians 2:8: *"By grace are ye saved through faith."*

The arch of salvation is all grace from the Godward side and all faith from the man-ward. God's grace is always perfect. But how imperfect is man's faith! Grace has provided in Christ all that is needed for a life of habitual spirituality. But to make such salvation experimental faith must appropriate the provision. Grace provides; faith possesses. Faith makes experimental what grace made potential to every believer.

God tells us that without faith it is impossible to please Him. Some of Christ's severest rebukes were to unbelief in His disciples. To have His presence, His words, His works fail to inspire faith grieved the Lord Jesus exceedingly.

You remember when He was in the ship and the storm arose and they cried out in fear. What a word of rebuke He spoke! Even though the tempest raged and the waves dashed high and

He was asleep—yet He was there. Why should they fear? Fear and faith are incompatible.

"And he saith unto them, *Why are ye fearful, O ye of little faith?* Then he arose, and rebuked the winds and the sea; and there was a great calm" (Matt. 8:26).

At another time Peter was walking on the water at the Lord's command. The wind became boisterous and Peter began to sink. But why should he doubt? Had not the Lord of the sea said, "Come," and did not the power of His protection accompany the command? Doubt and faith are irreconcilable. If we have doubt we haven't faith; if we have faith we haven't doubt.

"And immediately Jesus stretched forth his hand, and caught him, and said unto him, *O thou of little faith, wherefore didst thou doubt?*" (Matt. 14:31).

The disciples had crossed the lake after witnessing Christ feed the multitudes with a few loaves and fishes. They were greatly concerned because they had forgotten to take bread. Why should that cause worry? Had they not just seen Him feed more than four thousand people with seven loaves and a few fishes with seven baskets full left over? Would He not be equal to furnishing an evening meal for twelve people if need be? Worry and faith cannot dwell together.

"Which when Jesus perceived, he said unto them, *O ye of little faith, why reason ye among yourselves, because ye have brought no bread?* Do ye not understand, neither remember the five loves of the five thousand, and how many baskets ye took up? Neither the seven loaves of the four thousand, and how many baskets ye took up?" (Matt. 16:8-9).

Oh! how we crowd Him out of our lives by that triumvirate of evil—fear, doubt and worry! Failing health, financial losses, overwhelming burdens, tempests of affliction and adversity come upon us and we become insensible to His presence, doubt His Word and forget His works.

Some of Christ's sweetest words of commendation were called forth by faith, and strange to say they were spoken to those who knew Him the least. The centurion, whose servant lay sick, appealed to Christ to heal him. Christ promised to go to him. But the centurion answered, "Lord, *speak the word only* and my servant shall be healed." Oh! the joy such faith brought to Jesus' heart and the sweet commendation to His lip, "I have not found so great faith, no, not in Israel."

There is no record in God's Word and no instance in human experience where grace and love have failed to respond to faith and trust. God would be untrue to His nature, which is love, if He failed once to respond to real faith. To some of you such faith may seem impossible. But faith is the simplest thing in the world. Faith is just looking unto Jesus Christ and taking Him at His Word. Why isn't it easy then to have faith? It is because we look at the difficulties instead of Christ, and the more we look at them the bigger they become. They shut Christ out of our vision. Faith in itself has no power whatsoever to save or to keep us, but it links us to Christ who has the power. Let us now consider three ways in which faith operates.

Faith is Rooted in God's Great Facts

Walking along a wooded path in the mountains of Switzerland I saw an interesting tree. On a steep slope was a tall pine tree with a huge boulder lodged right underneath it, lifting the main trunk several feet from the ground. The tree was fairly sitting on top of the rock, yet it shot straight upward fifty feet. How could such a position be maintained? The secret was not hidden from our view. The roots of the tree had spread themselves over that rock and had gone down, deep, deep, into the earth around, so that even the boulder lodged at its very heart could not overturn or overwhelm it.

What a lesson it spoke! Afflictions, adversities, sufferings, sorrows, temptations, trials, doubts, disappointments roll in upon us. How can we go on in peace, patience and victory with such things in our life? Are they not enough to overwhelm us? No, not if faith spreads itself out over them and sends its roots down into the rich soil of God's great, eternal facts.

What are some of these facts? I can mention only a few to-night, but I hope you will search God's Word and find many more of them for yourself.

God is love.

"He that loveth not knoweth not God; for *God is love*." (I John 4:8).

This is one of the greatest of God's eternal facts, for us to root our faith in. It may seem as though God had forgotten or that His hand of chastening were too heavy upon you. It may seem as though He had closed His eyes or deafened His ear. It may even seem as though He were altogether indifferent to the burden you carry and the heartache you endure. But, friends, it isn't so, for God is love and the love of God shines as the brightness of the sun, whether you are warmed and refreshed by its rays or not.

A Chinese woman came to ask me why she couldn't win her mother, an ardent Buddhist, for whom she had prayed for years and whose heart had constantly grown harder. As I studied her face I saw lines which indicated hardness and rebellion in her own heart. With a little gentle probing there came a torrent of both tears and words. "God is unfair; He doesn't treat me right; other mothers can have their children but I have lost my five boys one by one; the last, my baby, died just last month. God is unfair." For a few moments we cried together and then we talked together of the love of God. That love had given the five boys; surely it was love that had taken them back home to Himself. Slowly the roots of that little woman's faith spread themselves over that boulder of sorrow and went down, down, down into this eternal fact "God is love." Then peace and joy came into her heart. "What has happened to you?" she said; "I never saw your face like this before." Then the daughter told her of the rebellion toward God but that now it was gone. From that day the mother was willing to hear the gospel and in a few weeks had accepted Christ as her Saviour.

God's Grace is Sufficient

"And he said unto me, *My grace is sufficient for thee:* for my strength is made perfect in weakness. Most gladly therefore will I rather glory in my infirmities, that the power of Christ may rest upon me." (II Cor. 12:9).

God never promised that the Christian would not have temptations and trials, but He did promise that with every temptation there would be a way of escape, and that with every trial there would be strength to endure. When our weakness is most pressing His strength is most perfect.

Christ is Able to Save to the Uttermost

Perhaps some of you said last night, "I cannot live a yielded life in Hong Kong." You thought of your non-Christian home, of your social circle with its gaiety and worldliness, of your business life with its temptations to dishonesty and graft, and you said, "I can't live a yielded life in such surroundings." Yes, you can if you let the roots of faith reach into the soil of this eternal fact, "Christ is able to save to the uttermost." He has both the power to cleanse from sin and to keep from sinning.

Think of the boulders that rolled in upon the life of the Apostle Paul: stripes, stonings, shipwreck, perils and persecutions of all kinds. But his faith spread itself over all these testings and trials and rooted itself in the eternal facts of God's love, grace and power, thus enabling him to grow up to magnificent spiritual stature. What the glorified Christ did for Paul He stands ready to do for you and me.

Faith Beckons on God's Faithfulness

Our faith may falter but His faithfulness never. Peter failed Christ, but Christ's faithfulness to Peter remained unshaken. The heavenly Father cannot forget His promises nor can He deny Himself by failing to keep them.

"If we are faithless, he abideth faithful; for he cannot deny himself." (II Tim. 2:13, R.V.).

We may be ready to give up in defeat to the enemy, to lay down our task in sheer discouragement or even to take our hand from the plough and turn back altogether. But Christ is not dismayed or discouraged. He will not give up in despair. He acknowledges no victory on the devil's part. He has assumed responsibility for us and He abideth faithful.

"Faithful is he that calleth you, who also will do it." (I Thess. 5:24).

In Switzerland I watched two girls cross a glacier. The path was not marked out; there were great gaping holes in the ice; they were not properly shod with spiked shoes. Yet they tripped along unafraid and in safety, because they were roped to one who knew how to avoid the dangers and surmount the difficulties of that icy path and they reckoned on the faithfulness of their guide.

Our pilgrim journey is beset with dangers and difficulties but we need have no fear for we, too, are roped to a Guide, who is especially appointed by our Father to lead us safely the entire way.

Faith Receives God's Fullness

Are you God's child? Then, by virtue of your sonship, you may be filled with the Spirit. Why, then, do you not possess your birthright? There are three ways an honest man may gain possession of a thing—by purchase, by barter or as a gift.

Can one buy the fullness of the Holy Spirit? Simon the sorcerer was severely rebuked for attempting it. Is there anything we can exchange with God for it? The rich young ruler might have exchanged half of his possessions for the life more abundant, but he went away sorrowful. Have you, perchance, tried to strike a bargain with God, offering Him some odd moments of time, some remnants of strength, some segment of talent, in exchange for the fullness of the Holy Spirit? One way remains by which you may possess the Holy Spirit's fullness, which is to receive it as a gift.

"And hereby we know that he abideth in us, *by the Spirit which he hath given us.*" (I John 3:24).

What does one usually do with a gift? He receives it and thanks the giver. This is precisely what God wants you to do with this wondrous gift of the Holy Spirit's fullness.

Let me illustrate by an incident which brought this truth to my own heart with fresh meaning. Two Chinese friends, Mr. and Mrs. Wang, came to call upon me one day. Mr. Wang was only a young Christian but he loved the Lord devotedly. What a love for the Word of God also! It was his meat and drink. Seeing this, I was reminded of a Scofield Bible some one had sent me to give to a Chinese friend. I presented it to Mr. Wang, saying, "I see you love the Bible. Here is a Scofield Bible which I should like to give you." At the mention of a Scofield Bible his face grew radiant and his eyes filled with tears. "Oh," said he, "the other day I saw a Scofield Bible and how I have wanted to possess one ever since! I began to pray for one. I went to a store to buy one but I couldn't afford it."

Mr. Wang decided he could not buy a Bible and no one had offered to exchange one for anything which he had. Just one way of possession was open to him—to receive it as a gift. And now it was being offered to him. What did he do?

Did he say, "I want that Bible more than anything but *I haven't prayed long enough for it*—just wait until I pray a few months more for it." Or, *"I am really not worthy* to receive that Bible. I must wait until I have made myself a better Christian and am worthy to possess it." Or, *"This Bible is coming too easily.* I think I should do something myself to get it." Or, "You say that Bible is for me but *I do not feel* that it is, so I think I should wait until I feel that I possess it."

If Mr. Wang had made any one of those foolish remarks I should have been forced to one of two conclusions; either he was not honest and really did not want a Scofield Bible or else he thought I was not honest in truly offering that one to him.

But what did Mr. Wang do? I wish you could have seen the quickness with which he TOOK that Bible and immediately kneeled down and THANKED God for it. As he rose he began to talk of how he would USE the gift in winning men to Christ.

Have you wanted the fullness of the Holy Spirit? God offers Him in His fullness to you as a gift. What have you done with the offer? Are you still praying for this fullness? Or are you refusing the gift until you think yourself worthy of it? Or are you foolishly attempting through self-effort to make yourself full of the Spirit? Or are you waiting for some ecstatic feeling as a proof of the infilling of the Spirit of God?

My friend, if you are telling God that you long to be filled with the Holy Spirit and yet doing these foolish things, either you are not honest and really do not want to be filled or else you do not believe that God is honest when He offers you the gift of the Spirit's fullness.

Are you honest? Do you truly want to be filled with the Holy Spirit? Then acknowledge the presence of the Holy Spirit within you and claim His fullness as your birthright. Take the gift, thank the Giver, and use the gift immediately in winning souls to Christ.

By an act of faith you may receive the Spirit's fullness. By a constant succession of acts of faith the Spirit's fullness becomes habitual. RIVERS OF LIVING WATER—pp. 111-124—Ruth Paxson.

THE FRUIT OF THE SPIRIT IS MEEKNESS

First Day.

Galatians 5:22-24: "But the fruit of the Spirit is love, joy, peace, longsuffering, kindness, goodness, faithfulness, meekness, self-control; against such there is no law. And they that are of Christ Jesus have crucified the flesh with the passions and the lusts thereof."

Since this is the eighth of a series of nine studies on the fruit of the Spirit, it might be well to review the material we have covered. It has been suggested that the nine elements in the fruit of the Spirit could be broken up into three divisions and applications as follows:

	(1)	Love
A. *Inward Fruit:*	(2)	Joy
	(3)	Peace
	(4)	Longsuffering
B. *Outward Fruit:*	(5)	Kindness
	(6)	Goodness
	(7)	Faithfulness
C. *Upward Fruit:*	(8)	Meekness
	(9)	Self-Control

Please notice the area of *meekness.* Is it not misplaced as some might feel—*meekness* is not in the outward or manward division —some might think so, but a careful definition of the term will teach us otherwise. What is meekness? Too many people equate it with weakness. Who was the meekest man on earth? Someone is so characterized in the Bible—who was it? Read Numbers 12:3. Would anyone accuse Moses of being weak?—and yet he was God's meekest man!

Second Day.

Numbers 12:1-3; 6-8: "And Miriam and Aaron spake against Moses because of the Cushite woman whom he had married; for he had married a Cushite woman. And they said, Hath Jehovah indeed spoken only with Moses? Hath he not spoken also with us? And Jehovah heard it. Now the man Moses was very meek, above all men that were upon the face of the earth. 6. And he said, Hear now my words: if there be a prophet among you, I Jehovah will make myself known unto him in a vision, I will speak with him in a dream. My servant Moses is not so; he is faithful in all my house: with him will I speak mouth to mouth, even manifestly, and not in dark speeches; and the form of Jehovah shall he behold: wherefore then were ye not afraid to speak against my servant, against Moses?"

Meekness is a reaction or a response given from the presence of God. Meekness is the outward expression of true reverence. Moses was not weak with man or God—see him:

1. As he kills the Egyptian and hides the body in the sand,
2. As he threw his rod down before Pharoah and demanded the release of the Hebrew slaves.
3. As he called forth the terrible plagues upon the land of Egypt,
4. As he called upon the whole nation of Israel to go forward into the Red Sea. But Moses was God's meek man—why? Because of his close communion with God. Meekness is the holy awe felt in our total being when we are aware of the presence of the Almighty God.

Is it now easier to understand why meekness is the fruit of the Holy Spirit? How we do need to practice an awareness of His presence within us. What does it mean to be the sanctuary of God? "Know ye not that your body is the temple of the Holy Spirit?" (I Cor. 6:19, 20). What sacred awe filled the heart of the high-priest as once a year he stepped into the sacred enclosure of the Holy of holies—the shekinah glory of God was the light of that room—such an experience filled the high-priest with meekness. If somehow we could pause long enough—and think deeply enough we would recognize the sacredness of God's sanctuary—we would see God's holy of holies on earth today—our bodies. The Almighty God of ten million universes has condescended to dwell in us through His Holy Spirit—considering our unworthiness and His greatness we should be meek indeed!

Third Day.

Exodus 3:1-6: "Now Moses was keeping the flock of Jethro his father-in-law, the priest of Midian: and he led the flock to the back of the wilderness, and came to the mountain of God, unto Horeb. And the angel of Jehovah appeared unto him in a flame of fire out of the midst of a bush: and he looked, and, behold, the bush burned with fire, and the bush was not consumed. And Moses said, I will turn aside now, and see this great sight, why the bush is not burnt. And when Jehovah saw that he turned aside to see, God called unto him out of the midst of the bush, and said, Moses, Moses. And he said, Here am I. And he said, Draw not nigh hither: put off thy shoes from off thy feet, for the place whereon thou standest is holy ground. Moreover he said, I am the God of thy Father, the God of Abraham, the God of Isaac, and the God of Jacob. And Moses hid his face; for he was afraid to look upon God."

Here we have the source of the meekness of Moses. We want to follow this man Moses out to the backside of the desert. There was no thing strange about the bush on fire—the unusual feature was that it was not consumed by the fire—he turned aside to investigate. Surely he was not prepared for the grand discovery. Moses expresses his meekness in action. He stood at a respectful distance from the presence of God—he removed the shoes from his feet—an act of humility. He hid his face for he was afraid. All of this and more we should feel as the sacred sanctuary of the Holy Spirit of God. A title appeared some years ago on the marquee of the theatre; it flashed off and on the words: *"Nothing Sacred."* This attitude of the world has been adopted by the children of God—as long as this is true there will be no meekness, for meekness begins with a sense of sacred respect. Putting off the shoes can be thought of as removing all filth or dirt from your person in the presence of God. (We are thinking of moral filth or defilement.) We cannot come into the presence of God with dirty minds or a soiled conscience. "Bow down before Him, love and adore Him, His name is Wonderful." In this reality the Holy Spirit has produced His fruit of meekness.

Fourth Day.

Matt. 11:28-30: "Come unto me, all ye that labor and are heavy laden, and I will give you rest. Take my yoke upon you, and learn of me; for I am meek and lowly in heart: and ye shall find rest unto your souls. For my yoke is easy, and my burden is light."

We have said all we have about Moses so we could better meditate on the prophet like unto Moses. He was *meek* and lowly in heart. It shall be our purpose to notice the elements of meekness as found in our Lord and ask God through the Holy Spirit to translate them into life—our life!

1. *Our Lord had no harshness or vindictiveness in carrying out the Father's will*—why?—because there is no harshness or vindictiveness in God and our Lord lived constantly conscious of the presence of God. We like Moses have been commissioned by God

138

to carry out His will; how do we do it?—or do we do it at all? Meekness presupposes the carrying out of the Father's will. We like Isaiah fall down in the presence of a Holy God and cry, "Woe is me for I am unclean." The next natural response is "What wilt thou have me to do."

2. *No attempt to force the will of God*—a gentle spirit of waiting on God is the spirit of meekness. We do not tell God when to move—He tells us! How we need this element of meekness. We wonder so often why our Lord seemed to be so leisurely about such an urgent mission. Why was He willing to stop amid a busy ministry to talk to little children? Why did He stop to heal the unnamed hundreds of poor folk who thronged His way? Because He moved under the compassionate heart and hand of God. He was meek and lowly in heart.

Fifth Day.

Matt. 21:5: "Tell ye the daughter of Zion, Behold, thy King cometh unto thee, Meek, and riding upon an ass, And upon a colt the foal of an ass."

We are not through with the qualities of meekness found in Jesus. (May it be said we are never through with these qualities until He is formed in our hearts.)

3. *No pomp or pride*—I have read of a king in the days of Esther: his name was Ahasuerus—see him sitting on his elaborately carved golden throne? By his people he is considered a superior being; some believe he is a god. None may come into the presence of this great king without an invitation. Should someone venture past the circle of guards, he will be cut down—that is unless the king raises his golden sceptre. Even Esther, his beloved, is afraid to draw near and must put her life in her hand to step into his presence.

But behold our king! Here he comes—the king of kings, the Lord of Lords—who are his guards?—they are unseen angels. Where is His army?—who are His attendants? See the children; they are His attendants—what are they saying? "Hosanna to the Son of David"—on what is He riding?—on the foal of an ass. His appointments are palm branches—his army the poor.

But we are kings and priests unto God. So many times we act much more like Ahasuerus than our meek and lowly Lord. Please remember that *all our authority is delegated.* "Nothing I have but what was given to me."

4. *Meekness makes one approachable.* Once again watch our wonderful Lord. It happened in one of the brief and busy days of our Lord's life on earth: a group of mothers leading and carrying their children came to our Lord to seek an audience with Him. If our Lord had been like many of us, He would have been vexed that these small ignorant ones were going to interrupt His busy and important schedule with their trifles. If He responded like man and not like God He might have given them the cold shoulder of indifference. The disciples anticipated this (so called natural) response and started to rebuke the women and children for interrupting. But Jesus was different. He was meek. He was approachable. He said "let the children come unto me and forbid them not for to such belongs the kingdom of heaven."

Sixth Day.

Matt. 5:5: "Blessed are the meek: for they shall inherit the earth."

One more quality of meekness:

5. *Meekness removes all selfishness.* Please refer back to the definition of meekness and see how utterly impossible it is to be selfish and still be meek. What a strange paradox that the meek —the unselfish are promised the inheritance of the earth! We like the comment of Albert Barnes so well, we reproduce it here for our edification:

Meekness is patience in the reception of injuries. It is neither meanness nor a surrender of our rights, nor cowardice; but it is the opposite of sudden anger, of malice, of long-harboured vengeance. Christ insisted on his right when he said, "If I have done evil, bear witness of the evil; but if well, why smitedst thou me? John xviii. 23. Paul asserted his right when he said, "They have beaten us openly uncondemned, being Romans, and have cast us into prison; and now do they thrust us out privily? nay, verily; but let them come themselves, and fetch us out," Acts xvi. 37. And yet Christ was the very model of meekness. It was one of his characteristics, "I am meek" Matt. xi. 29. So of Paul. No man endured more wrong, or endured it more patiently than he. Yet the Saviour and the apostle were not passionate. They bore all patiently. They did not press their rights through thick and thin, or trample down the rights of others to secure their own.

Meekness is the reception of injuries with a belief that God will vindicate us. "Vengeance is his; he will repay," Rom. xii. 19. It little becomes us to take his place, and to do what he has promised to do.

Meekness produces peace. It is proof of true greatness of soul. It comes from a heart too great to be moved by little insults. It looks upon those who offer them with pity. He that is constantly ruffled; that suffers every little insult or injury to throw him off his guard and to raise a storm of passion within, is at the mercy of every mortal that chooses to disturb him. He is like "the troubled sea that cannot rest, whose waters cast up mire and dirt."

They shall inherit the earth. This might have been translated the land. It is probable that here is a reference to the manner in which the Jews commonly expressed themselves to denote any great blessing. It was promised to them that they should inherit the land of Caanan. For a long time the patriarchs looked forward to this, Gen. xv. 7, 8; Exo. xxxii. 13. They regarded it as a great blessing. It was so spoken of in the journey in the wilderness, and their hopes were crowned when they took possession of the promised land. Deut. i. 38; xvi. 20. In the time of our Saviour they were in the constant habit of using the Old Testament, where this promise perpetually occurs, and they used it as a proverbial expression to denote any great blessing, perhaps as the sum of all blessings, Ps. xxxvii. 20; Is. lx. 21. Our Saviour used it in this sense, and meant to say, not that the meek would own great property or have many lands, but that they would possess peculiar blessings. The Jews also considered the land of Caanan as a type of heaven, and of the blessings under the Messiah. To inherit the land became, therefore, an expression denoting those blessings. When our Saviour uses this language here, he means that the meek shall be received into his kingdom, and partake of its blessings here, and of the glories of the heavenly Caanan hereafter.—The value of meekness, even in regard to worldly property and success in life, is often exhibited in the Scriptures, Pro. xxii. 24, 25; xv. 1; xxv. 8, 15. It is also seen in common life that a meek, patient, mild man is the most prospered. An impatient and quarrelsome man raises up enemies; often loses property in lawsuits; spends his time in disputes and broils rather than in sober, honest industry; and is harassed, vexed, and unsuccessful in all that he does. "Godliness is profitable unto all things, having promise of the life that now is, and of that which is to come," I Tim. iv. 8. Comp. I. Tim. vi. 3-6. FROM BARNES' NOTES ON THE NEW TESTAMENT by Albert Barnes, pp. 44, 45.

Seventh Day.

I Peter 3:1-4; 15: "In like manner, ye wives, be in subjection to your own husbands; that, even if any obey not the word, they may without the word be gained by the behavior of their wives; beholding your chaste behavior coupled with fear. Whose adorning let it not be the outward adorning of braiding the hair, and of wearing jewels of gold, or of putting on apparel; but let it be the hidden man of the heart, in the incorruptible apparel of a meek and quiet spirit, which is in the sight of God of great price. 15. But sanctify in your hearts Christ as Lord: being ready always to give answer to every man that asketh you a reason concerning the hope that is in you, yet with meekness and fear:" James 1:21 "Wherefore putting away all filthiness and overflowing of wickedness, receive with meekness the implanted word, which is able to save your souls."

Here are instructions for all in the area of meekness. What an ornament—what an adornment is meekness. Please notice the influence meekness will have upon the total person. As a garment covers the body in such a manner that we see nothing but the garment, so does the virtue of meekness when we let it assert its influence over us. Both in the sight of man and God, a meek and quiet spirit is much to be desired.

The beautiful process of developing meekness is pointed out in I Pet. 3:15. "Set Christ aside in your heart," i.e., make a conscious effort to let Christ dominate your thoughts, your will, your conscience, your affections. But what reaction do we have from His indwelling power and presence?—One of holy awe or reverence. When called upon to defend our faith or to answer for Him, we are always ready to give an answer and with the right attitude— one proceeding from an awareness of His majesty and beauty in "meekness and fear."

Consider carefully James 1:21. Without the casting off as a dirty garment all filthiness and overflowing of maliciousness, we cannot and will not be prepared to receive with meekness the life giving word—without meekness the Word of God is a dead letter and our souls are lost as a consequence. Meekness is not only nice it is necessary!

Comment For The Week
LIKE CHRIST IN MEEKNESS
By Andrew Murray

It is on His way to the cross that we find the first of these two words written of our Lord Jesus. It is in His sufferings that the meekness of Jesus is specially manifested. Follower of Jesus, who art so ready to take Thy place under the shadow of His cross, there to behold the Lamb slain for thy sins, is it not a precious thought, that there is one part of His work, as the suffering Lamb of God, in which thou mayst bear His image and be like Him every day? Thou canst be meek and gentle even as He was.

Meekness is the opposite of all that is hard or bitter or sharp. It has reference to the disposition which animates us towards our inferiors. "With meekness," ministers must instruct those that oppose themselves, teach and bring back the erring (Gal. vi. 1; II Tim ii. 25). It expresses our disposition towards our superiors: we must "receive the word with meekness" (Jas. 1. 21); if the wife is to be in subjection to her husband, it must be in a meek and quiet spirit, which is in the sight of God of great price (I Pet. iii). As one of the fruits of the Spirit, meekness ought to characterize all our daily intercourse with fellow Christians, and extend to all with whom we have to do (Eph. iv. 2; Gal. v. 22; Col. iii. 12; Tit. iii. 2). It is mentioned in Scripture along with humility, because that is the inward disposition concerning oneself, out of which meekness towards others springs.

There is perhaps none of the lovely virtues which adorn the image of God's Son, which is more seldom seen in those who ought to be examples. There are many servants of Jesus, in whom much love to souls, much service for the salvation of others, and much zeal for God's will are visible, and yet who continually come short in this. How often, when offence comes unexpectedly, whether at home or abroad, they are carried away by temper and anger, and have to confess that they have lost the perfect rest of soul in God! There is no virtue, perhaps, for which some have prayed more earnestly; they feel they would give anything, if in their intercourse with partner, or children, or servants, in company or in business, they could always keep their temper perfectly, and exhibit the meekness and gentleness of Christ. Unspeakable is the grief and disappointment experienced by those who have learned to long for it, and yet have not discovered where the secret of meekness lies.

The self-command needed for this seems to some so impossible, that they seek comfort in the belief that this blessing belongs to a certain natural temperament, and is too contrary to their character for them ever to expect it. To satisfy themselves they find all sorts of excuses. They do not mean it so ill; though the tongue or the temper be sharp, there is still love in their hearts; it would not be good to be too gentle, evil would be strengthened by it. And thus the call to entire conformity to the holy gentleness of the Lamb of God is robbed of its power. And the world is strengthened in its belief that Christians are after all not very much different from other people, because, though they do indeed say, they do not show, that Christ changes the heart and life after His own image. And the soul suffers itself, and causes unspeakable harm in Christ's Church, through its unfaithfulness in appropriating this blessing of salvation, the bearing the image and likeness of God.

This grace is of great price in the sight of God. In the Old Testament there are many glorious promises for the meek, which were by Jesus gathered up into this one, "Blessed are the meek, for they shall inherit the earth" (see Ps. xxv. 9; lxxvi. 9; Prov. iii. 34; Jer. ii. 3). In the New Testament, its praise consists in this, that it is His meekness that gives its supernatural incomparable beauty to the image of our Lord. A meek spirit is of great price in God's sight; it is the choicest ornament of the Beloved Son. The Father could surely offer no higher inducement to His children, to seek it above all things.

For every one who longs to possess this spirit, Christ's word is full of comfort and encouragement: "Learn of me that I am meek." And what will it profit us to learn that *He is meek?* Will not just the experience of His meekness make the discovery of our want of it all the more painful? What we ask, Lord, is that Thou shouldst teach us how *we* may be meek. The answer is again: "Learn of *me* that I AM MEEK."

144

How Can I Have the Fruit of the Spirit?

We are in danger of seeking meekness and the other graces of our Lord as gifts of which we must be conscious, before we practice them.

This is not the path of faith. "Moses knew not that his face shone"; he had only seen the glory of God. The soul that seeks to be meek must learn that Jesus is meek. We must take time to gaze on His meekness, until the heart has received the full impression: He only is meek; with Him alone can meekness be found. When we begin to realize this, we next fix our hearts upon the truth: This meek one is *Jesus the Saviour.* All He is, all He has, is for His redeemed ones; His meekness is to be communicated to us. But He does not impart it by giving, as it were, from Himself, something of it away to us. No; we must learn that He alone is meek, and that only when He enters and takes possession of heart and life, He brings His meekness with Him. It is with the meekness of Jesus that we can be meek.

We know how little He succeeded in making His disciples meek and lowly while on earth. It was because He had not yet obtained the new life, and could not yet bestow, through His resurrection, the Holy Spirit. But now He can do it. He has been exalted to the power of God, from thence to reign in our hearts, to conquer every enemy, and continue in us His own holy life. Jesus was our visible Example on earth, that we might see in Him what like the hidden life is that He would give us from Heaven, that He himself would be within us.

"Learn of me, for I am meek and lowly of heart"; without ceasing the word sounds in our ears as our Lord's answer to all the sad complaints of His redeemed ones, as to the difficulty of restraining temper. O my brother, why is Jesus your Jesus, your life, and your strength; why is He the meek and lowly One, if it be not to impart to you, to whom He so wholly belongs, His own meekness?

Therefore, only believe! Believe that Jesus is able to fill your heart with His own Spirit of meekness. Believe that Jesus Himself will, through His own Spirit, accomplish in you the work that you have in vain endeavoured to do. "BEHOLD! THY KING COMETH TO THEE MEEK." Welcome Him to dwell in your heart. Expect Him to *reveal Himself to you.* Everything depends on this. Learn of Him that He is meek and lowly of heart, and you shall find rest to your soul.

145

Precious Saviour, grant me now, under the overshadowing of Thy Holy Spirit, to draw near unto Thee, and to appropriate Thy heavenly meekness as my life. Lord, Thou hast not shown me Thy meekness as a Moses who demands, but does not give. Thou art Jesus, who savest from all sin, giving in its stead Thy heavenly holiness. Lord, I claim Thy meekness as a part of the salvation that Thou hast given me. I cannot do without it. How can I glorify Thee if I do not possess it? Lord, I will learn from Thee that Thou art meek. Blessed Lord, teach me. And teach me that Thou art always with me, always in me as my life. Abiding in Thee, with Thee abiding in me, I have Thee, the meek One, to help me and make me like Thyself.

O holy meekness, Thou art not come down to earth only for a short visit, then to disappear again in the heavens. Thou art come to seek a home. I offer Thee my heart; come and dwell in it.

Thou blessed Lamb of God, my Saviour and Helper, I count on Thee. Thou wilt make Thy meekness to dwell in me. Through Thy indwelling Thou dost conform me to Thy image. Oh, come, and as an act of Thy rich, free grace, even now, as I wait on Thee, reveal Thyself as my King, meek, and coming in to take possession of me for Thyself.

> "Precious, gentle, holy Jesus,
>   Blessed Bridegroom of my heart,
> In Thy secret inner chamber,
>   Thou wilt show me *what Thou art*." Amen.

From LIKE CHRIST by Andrew Murray, pp. 212-218.

THE FRUIT OF THE SPIRIT IS SELF-CONTROL

First Day.

Galatians 5:22, 23: "But the fruit of the Spirit is love, joy, peace, longsuffering, kindness, goodness, faithfulness, meekness, *self-control:* against such there is no law." Phil. 3:3. "For we are the circumcision, who worship by the Spirit of God, and glory in Christ Jesus, and have no confidence in the flesh:" Rom. 7:18. "For I know that in me, that is, in my flesh, dwelleth no good thing: for to will is present with me, but to do that which is good is not."

Upon surface consideration there seems to be a contradiction of terms. We are told to have no confidence in the flesh—to believe that in the flesh there is no ability to overcome the power of Satan. We are urged "to crucify the flesh"—"to put to death the deeds of the body." And yet we are told we are able to control self! Please read the text again. *"The fruit of the Spirit is self-control."* The emphasis is upon the Spirit not upon self. We of ourselves, apart from His help, can do nothing.

In a very real sense to have either the first or the last of the elements of the fruit of the Spirit is to have all of them. To have love includes all others: If the Holy Spirit is in control of the self-life; then love, joy, peace, longsuffering, kindness, goodness, and meekness are all ours also. "But," someone says, "how can the Holy Spirit control my inner-self?" The answer is easy but the *appropriation* is not. *The Holy Spirit can control your self-life when you are willing to turn yourself over to Him.*

But this does not really answer the need. We cannot follow the will of the Holy Spirit unless we know what He wants us to do. We can find His will in the life of our Lord. To submit yourself to the life and teachings of our Lord is to submit yourself to the Holy Spirit for they are in relationship to us, one and the same person. Our purpose then is the same as it has been from the beginning of this study—to discover the control of the self-life by our Lord and ask the Holy Spirit to enable us to make this a personal reality.

Second Day.

Hebrews 2:17, 18: "Wherefore it behooved him in all things to be made like unto his brethren, that he might become a merciful and faithful high priest in things pertaining to God, to make propitiation for the sins of the people. For in that he himself hath suffered being tempted, he is able to succor them that are tempted."

Hebrews 4:15, 16: "For we have not a high priest that cannot be touched with the feeling of our infirmities; but one that hath been in all points tempted like as we are, yet without sin. Let us therefore draw near with boldness unto the throne of grace, that we may receive mercy, and may find grace to help us in time of need."

It is such a comforting thought to know our Lord was "in *all things* to be made like unto his brethren,"—to read that we have one "that hath been in *all points tempted like as we are,* yet without sin." The weapons of His warfare with Satan are available to you and me. Jesus faced our common adversary "in the likeness of sinful flesh"—and overcame as an example for us that "we should walk in His steps, who knew no sin."

Read again Hebrews 2:18 with emphasis upon the phrase "he himself *hath suffered being tempted,*"—our problem is not with temptation alone but with the inevitable suffering that accomplishes it.

Read I Cor. 10:13. "There hath no temptation taken you but such as is common to man: but God is faithful, who will not suffer you to be tempted above that ye are able; but will with the temptation also make a way of escape, that ye may be able to bear it."

We do not want to endure temptation; we want to triumph over it in some painless victory that would give far more glory to ourselves than God. God has given us a way of escape with every temptation that we may be able to *"endure it."* There is no lesson of appreciation in overcoming temptation if there is no suffering in the temptation and victory. If we are looking for help from the Holy Spirit in overcoming temptation minus suffering and a trial of mind and nerves, we would not be like our blessed Lord who overcame *through suffering.*

Third Day.

Matthew 4:1-4: "Then was Jesus led up of the Spirit into the wilderness to be tempted of the devil. And when he had fasted forty days and forty nights, he afterward hungered. And the tempter came and said unto him, If thou art the Son of God, command that these stones become bread. But he answered and said, It is written, Man shall not live by bread alone, but by every word that proceedeth out of the mouth of God."

How is it that the Holy Spirit led our Saviour into the wilderness to be tempted? It is no sin to be tempted—indeed if we did not have the capacity to be tempted there would be a fatal flaw in our nature, for we would be no longer in the image of God—i.e., we would no longer have the power of choice. How shall we demonstrate the genuineness of anything or anyone without a test? We can expect the Holy Spirit to accompany us and even to lead us in the tests and trials of this wilderness journey.

We want to point out but two truths in this exercise of self-control by our Lord: (1) this was a temptation to *"the flesh,"* to satisfy the appetite of the physical body. There is nothing wrong in such a desire; it is part of the God given desire of self-preservation—the problem is always in *how* this desire will be satisfied. There are at least two basic expressions of this desire: food and sex. Will we use food or be used by food—will we control the sex-urge or become a slave to it?

(2) In the second place the temptation of Jesus was to use His divine power selfishly—so many of our choices have the element of selfishness in them. There is so much attempt at *self*-confidence, *self*-esteem, *self*-indulgence, *self*-congratulation, *self*-righteousness, *self*-complaining, *self*-reflection.

Control was exercised in satisfying the desire of the flesh as master of the desire and not mastered by it.

Control was exercised in rejecting the desire to be selfish with the abilities granted by God.

Fourth Day.

Matthew 4:5-7: "Then the devil taketh him into the holy city; and he set him on the pinnacle of the temple, and saith unto him, If thou art the Son of God, cast thyself down: for it is written, He shall give his angels charge concerning thee: and, On their hands they shall bear thee up, Lest haply thou dash thy foot against a stone. Jesus said unto him, Again it is written, Thou shalt not make trial of the Lord thy God."

The request in these verses was to ask God to suspend His divine laws to protect His son from suffering. This would have been a legitimate request if vain-glory was not included in the request. The answer was to include a showy demonstration of Divine power. Satan here offered a short-cut to the acceptance of His divinity. How subtle a temptation is this. How often we are tempted to take a short-cut to what we know is God's will. Jesus knew it was the Father's will that all men believe He was the Son of God—but such acceptance could not be obtained in the way Satan offered. Let's look at some short cuts of Satan in our lives: (1) *"Every* branch that beareth fruit *He cleanseth it* that it may bear *more fruit."* John 15:2. We all want to bear more fruit but not all of us want to produce it through cleansing. There are various painless short cuts to more fruit. Is there some other way to produce the virtues in our character apart from suffering? This text says *every branch* must be pruned before it can bear more fruit. (2) "Tribulation worketh steadfastness." Rom. 5:3. Is there some other way to develop steadfastness?

Mark out the areas of self-control in the life of our Lord:

(1) The course of the desire to resist or reject the cleansing

(1) The course of the desire to resist or reject the cleansing hand of the vine dresser, the Father.

(2) The control of resentment at undeserved tribulations, (that were although undeserved working steadfastness).

Fifth Day.

Luke 11:21-26: "When the strong man fully armed guardeth his own court, his goods are in peace: but when a stronger than he shall come upon him, and overcome him, he taketh from him his whole armor wherein he trusted, and divideth his spoils. He that is not with me is against me; and he that gathereth not with me scattereth. The unclean spirit when he is gone out of the man, passeth through waterless places, seeking rest, and finding none, he saith, I will turn back unto my house whence I came out. And when he is come, he findeth it swept and garnished. Then goeth he, and taketh to him seven other spirits more evil than himself; and they enter in and dwell there: and the last state of that man becometh worse than the first."

There are two or three wonderful lessons on the control of self found in these verses: (1) Reading these verses in their context we understand the "strong man" of verse twenty-one is Satan. The "stronger man" is our Lord through the "finger of God" or the "Holy Spirit." (Cf vs. 14-20.) The overcoming of Satan by the Holy Spirit was in the form of casting out a demon. At times we are caused to wonder if we or others are not in our day influenced by demons. Surely we have help from Satan in our thoughts and actions. Even if there was demon possession now, we could be delivered by "the finger of God" of the Holy Spirit. He is the only force to overcome and cast out Satanic power. (2) The second lesson is just as important as the first. There is no final victory over Satan. There is a continual triumph but no one single decisive battle that stands for all time and eternity. Please notice that it was just as important to guard and fill the house as it was to cleanse it in the first place. Restlessness is a characteristic of the demon—he must find an avenue—a means of expressing his pent-up energy. When he approaches our heart, he must find us already too busy and full of work for our Lord for him to obtain our attention or interest. If we are idle, or worse yet, engaged in some area of Satanic interest, he can come into our lives in seven-fold strength.

Sixth Day.

Matt. 12:34, 35: "Ye offspring of vipers, how can ye, being evil, speak good things? for out of the abundance of the heart the mouth speaketh. The good man out of his good treasure bringeth forth good things: and the evil man out of his evil treasure bringeth forth evil things."

We *are* responsible for the content of our hearts! The heart is a treasure-chest. The filling of the treasure-chest is the inalienable right of each person. No one is to say someone else filled his treasure while he was not aware of it. If we have no good words, kind words, patient words to say it is because of the heart's content. If we have not followed our Lord with our emotional nature—if we have not developed a conscience in the areas just mentioned; we have failed to exercise the self-control necessary to give us a good treasure (heart) out of which we can draw good things. We are evil because we want to be evil; we love the "pleasures of sin"; we have so controlled our time, thought and energies that we have produced an evil heart. Of course, we had the help of Satan in such an effort, but *we* were the *controlling factor!* We have the promised aid of the Holy Spirit in developing a good treasure (heart) and again we are the *controlling factor. "Keep thy heart with all diligence"*—please, please, notice *who* is to do the *keeping.*

Seventh Day.

Mark 3:13, 14: "And he goeth up into the mountain, and calleth unto him who he himself would; and they went unto him. And he appointed twelve, that they might be with him, and that he might send them forth to preach—."

Read again the fourteenth verse. Mark carefully the connection of being with Christ and going forth to preach. Had the twelve not been with Him, they would never have gone forth to declare His message. What does this have to do with "self-control?" It is the very crux of the whole matter. "Character is transformed by the influence of our fellowships. No man can become good merely by trying. A deepening character is generally the unconscious result of consciously chosen influences." (H.E.F.) When will you devotionally memorize the four gospels? When will you write your own commentary on the epistles? When will you establish a new church in a virgin territory? These are the choices that develop this virtue. You cannot memorize the gospels without self-control, but you can choose to do so and in the process develop both the capacity and virtue. This is true of your personal study of the epistles. You will never control self by yourself, but you can put yourself in a context of divine circumstances that God can work together for the production of this quality. Will you do it?

Comment For The Week
SELF-CONTROL
By Dr. A. T. Pierson

REGULATION OF THOUGHT

"For as he thinketh in his heart, so is he" (Proverbs 23:7).

As to the power to think, we know not which is more overwhelming, the grandeur of the ability or the awfulness of the responsibility. The endowment is itself a tie of kinship with the Infinite, and its exercise suggests infinity and eternity.

To think is to shape character and conduct. The mystic chambers where thought abides are the secret workshop of an unseen Sculptor, chiselling living forms for a deathless future. Personality and influence are modeled there. Hence the injunction, "Keep thy heart with all diligence; for out of it are the issues of life" (Prov. 4:23).

From many points of view the importance of regulating our thoughts is apparent. For example, meditation is simply thought prolonged and directed to a single class of objects. Of what vast consequence is it whether such meditation is fixed on what is pure, true, guileless, elevated, or what is defiling, debasing, degrading! How sure an index of what one really is at heart would be supplied if the character of his habitual meditations were known! For as a man "thinketh in his heart, so is he."

Our meditations also determine what we are becoming—growing to be. Thought has an assimilating power; its subjects and objects, whether sensibly or insensibly, mould us. What is first an idea becomes an image, then an ideal. If too low and mean to kindle enthusiasm or inspire emulation, it still wields a subtle influence, even while intellectually and morally it is disapproved.

Meditation is aided by imagination—the power of imaging forth. This is the soul's eye—the intellectual vision. The outer eye may be closed or blinded, but the image of what has been seen reappears at will, the memory assisting to recall and reproduce. Every image, therefore, set before the mind's eye is a creation of the imagination. Hence its grand imperial function in the sphere of art, impossible without it. Where had been Bunyan's immortal allegory, or Milton's celestial poem, or Michelangelo's *Moses* or *Cathedral,* or Bierstadt's *Yosemite,* but for this creative power? Capt. Eades said to the builders of his great bridge across the "Father of Waters": "I saw the bridge before the first caisson was sunk." Every work of the mechanic or of fine arts is first created in the mind, before pen or pencil or tool has begun its work.

Not less vital are thought, meditation, and imagination to holy living. Lofty or low, elevating or degrading, ideas and images *will* occupy the thinking powers and become sources of high purpose and endeavour, or of debasing and destructive aims and actions. A man's habits of thought both *forecast* and *cast* the character; they are its matrix and mould. If he dreams of power and position, he will become more and more ambitious and selfish; if he dreams of money, grasping and greedy; if of pleasure, sensual and carnal. His imagination may prove only dreams that never take shape in reality; he may be disappointed in attainment or achievement, but what he has sought, even though he fails, leaves ineffaceable traces on character. To the images and ideas on which his mind's eye is fixed he will be assimilated—whether to the miser or to the giver, the sinner or the saint, the devil or God.

> "But he that hides a dark soul and foul thoughts,
> Benighted walks under the midday sun,
> Himself in his own dungeon."
> —John Milton.

We must, therefore, go back to the thought life for the mould in which the man takes shape. Conduct essentially springs from character, and character from thought. The mouth speaks out of the abundance of the heart, and so speech takes its utterance from this secret, inner self. God therefore "looketh on the heart." He weighs the thoughts for His estimate of the man. He values purity of thought. Man is apt, in aiming at improvement, and even sanctity, to forget this hidden realm; to cultivate morals and manners, and be satisfied with the absence of open misconduct. But no life is pure in God's eyes where thought is not kept from evil; unguarded thoughts, sooner or later, find their way to the lips and outer life. The same prayer that asks to be kept back from "presumptuous sins" seeks "meditation of heart" that is acceptable in God's sight (Psalm 19:13, 14).

But, even if thought and conduct could be separated, are not evil thoughts, in themselves, as sinful as any other forms of evil, violations of law antagonistic to Him who is a Spirit? They may not affect our fellow men as much as our words and works, but they affect ourselves and our relations with God. Every cherished thought or motive of wrong is a blow dealt as in His face. Here in the thought life ideals or idols are first set up, and here is determined to what our allegiance is given. Here is the abyss none can bridge, the unfathomable, impassable gulf by which souls are distinguished and divided. Selfish motives often curb wrongdoing, but in this hidden realm, where human law does not restrain, nor human observation reach, we must find the real man.

We venture to hint some rules for godly self-control in the thought life:

Of course, all that verges on impurity must be sedulously avoided. This is axiomatic. Nothing can more offend God and degrade us than a foul imagination. If we walk in the Spirit, such images cannot be tolerated, much less cherished. Holy living and pure thinking are vitally linked.

So should frivolity be avoided. It may be an honest question whether in this harp of many strings humour is not one, and as such to contribute its chord to the melody and harmony of our being. There are times when a stern sobriety may relax in cheerful and mirthful moods. But to run wild in frolic, risks trampling on sacred territory, and crushing the bloom of the Spirit. A seemly mirth will wear the bit and bridle, and the reins will be kept in hand, otherwise liberty will run into license, and overstep right limits.

Moreover, in habitual levity lurks sin. It lessens, and finally destroys even the power of earnest sobriety and solemnity. And experience proves it true that when "the beginning of the words of his mouth is foolishness," then "the end of his talk" is often "mischievous madness" (Eccles. 10:13). When jesting becomes a habit, it seldom stops short of irreverence and indecency.

But we need a positive occupation of thought with high and holy themes—the expulsive power of a new and nobler affection. No man can long *keep out* evil who does not *keep in* good. An idle heart is the devil's workshop, but a mind preoccupied with heavenly things has no room for him. We must not only pray, "Search me, O God, try my thought," but bring into captivity every thought to the obedience of Christ (II Cor. 10:5); and "whatsoever things are true, honest, just, pure, lovely, of good report, THINK ON THESE THINGS."

REGULATION OF THE AFFECTIONS

"Set your affection on things above, not on things on the earth" (Collossians 3:2).

The faculties of thinking and feeling differ. We associate thought with the head and feeling with heart; and, perhaps, there is a scientific accuracy in the Bible use of the word "bowels" to indicate that the seat of the emotions lies in the vital organs. While it is true that brain activity affects the circulatory centers, and changes of pulsation respond sympathetically to the mental operations, we have learned that there is a solar plexus, or "abdominal brain," that is more closely connected with what we call emotion—the moving impulse. To say no more, the heart, with its warm blood currents, well suggests the ardour and fervour of feeling.

Thinking is the activity of the mind, in respect to ideas and facts, and implies no necessary movement of attraction or repulsion. But feeling, emotion, affection all express such movement, either by way of satisfaction or dissatisfaction, complacence or abhorrence. For example, two faces are seen which call up different associations: one, connected with falsehood, treachery, cruelty; the other, with kindness, generosity, nobility. When the mind has done its work in recognition and recollection, the feelings and emotions respond; there is a moving toward, or away from what is seen.

155

Some experiences lie on the borderland of thought and feeling, and might be called intellectual emotions; as when, interested in a poem or picture simply as a work of art or genius, the mind glows with enthusiasm over it. Here is something akin to loving, yet it scarcely belongs to the realm of the affections, as will appear so soon as we compare the effects upon us of looking at a marble statue and a mother's face!

We are now to consider, briefly, the regulation of the affections, which may include the feelings and emotions, but are deeper and more abiding. Emotions come and go with their exciting cause, as when suffering kindles emotions of sympathy and pity. Affection is an habitual bent toward an object—a permanent attitude and habitude, not dependent upon the presence of its object for its existence or persistence. Hence, however, important to control feeling and emotion, it is of vital consequence to regulate these deeper outgoings of the heart life, which are the index of character and the forecast of destiny.

Paul wrote to the Colossians not only to think on things above, but to set their affections on them—to seat them there, as Christ is seated at the right hand of God. We need to be permanently inclined, disposed in this heavenly direction; to fix our affections, like clinging tendrils, upon God; having in Him a personal Object around whom to twine, and in whom to find both satisfaction and support. Such seeking of things above implies deliberate withdrawal of affection from lower objects, and transfer of desire and delight, preference and purpose, to the higher. Nothing lower than God and Heaven deserves to be central and controlling.

To appreciate the importance of this, we must feel the dignity and power of the affections. The climax of God's self-given titles is "God is love." Power, even when infinite, awakens only awe; but infinite Love subdues, melts, wins. Grace stirs the whole being with gratitude, and floods it with tenderness. So, when God would most move us, He overwhelms us with visions of a Love so divine that it is not an attribute of God, but the equivalent of God. He is not merely loving and lovable, but is Love itself.

Our affections both reveal what character essentially is, and forecast what it is to be—even more than our thoughts, for the affections largely prompt our thought habits, determining what images we love to contemplate. The essence both of sin and holiness is largely here; for the acts both of sin and saintliness could have little moral quality were there no moral preference behind them. It is the love of evil which makes sin so damning, and the love of holiness which is the heart of sainthood. But for this heart affection for evil, how could the imagination be employed as sin's artist, or memory as its treasure gatherer, or the will as its marshal? But for this, even the Devil's hook would be bare of bait, and his wiles would find no response in us, as they found none in our tempted Master.

The carnal mind—the minding of the flesh, which is enmity against God, and the minding of the Spirit, which is life and peace—what are these but the habitual trend of the affections, one way or the other? How can one be subject to the law of God, who does not surrender to His love? Grace aims to implant and then nourish godly affections. They that are Christ's have crucified the fleshly affections and lusts, and buried them in His sepulchre, that in newness of life—resurrection life—heaven-born affections might take their place.

Our affections also determine our influence. What moves men is not mind so much as heart. The world over, the most potent force is not thought, but love. Argument often convinces while affection sways in a contrary direction. A teacher's wisdom, with all the fascinations of the schools, moves us less than a mother's pleading and tears. Even where masses of men bow before eloquent oratory, it is the power of sincerity and earnestness in the speaker that moves even those who differ. We all instinctively feel that the secret of heroism is noble affection, unselfish love, and sacrifice. There is a sort of righteousness that awakens only a cold admiration, while goodness, which is righteousness touched with love, leads men to die for its possessor.

Of course, what goes so far to mould character and shape influence, must determine destiny. When the great judicial scales of the Universal Judge are at last hung, it cannot be otherwise than that the central affections should settle which way those scales preponderate. What we have most truly loved must have vital connection with the eternal future—not only with the entrance into Heaven, but the capacity for its joys.

The same law that bids us set our affection on things above forbids us to fix them on things below. Earthly things are, in the

Scriptures, divided into two classes: what is in itself sinful, and what is relatively worthless. The former is always wrong; the latter is wrong when it becomes absorbing and idolatrous.

As to things sinful, there is but one course—immediate and complete renunciation. Obedience to God brooks neither delay nor compromise. One of the surest ways to mortify godless affections is to cease all parley with sin and make no provision for the flesh —to leave no room or quarter for the foe. If God is to occupy the fortress, the enemy must unconditionally surrender and immediately evacuate. For known sin God has no toleration. It is to be at once and for ever given up. There will always be left quite enough unknown, unrecognized sin.

But frivolities are unworthy of a child of God. Life is too solemn and earnest to be occupied with follies, inanities, and vanities. Surely we can spend time better than chasing baubles or blowing soap bubbles. The fashion of this world passeth away. That ought to be enough for him who, doing the will of God, abideth for ever. It pains us when we hear a doubting soul even asking, "May I do this or that?" The fact that a question arises should settle it. "Whatsoever is not of faith is sin." To indulge what is doubtful because not distinctly forbidden is to give inclination the preference over absolute loyalty to Him.

God leaves some things outside the pale of prohibition, partly to test us whether, in a matter of doubt, we will give Him or ourselves the advantage of the doubt! So long as the passing pleasures and pleasantries of this world, its follies and frivolities, its gaieties and gaudiness, sway us, our affections are not dislodged from lower things and seated with Christ in the heavenlies. A higher experience of transferred affections will change these vanities into vexations to the spirit. One of the surest signs of a holy life is the weaning of the child of God from the breast of the world.

Lower forms, even of good, may become evil by disproportionate attention and affection. The three lusts—avarice, appetite, and ambition—are all fallen angels. Originally they were simply the capacity for increase, for pleasure, and for advancement. They represent perversion through excess, means turned to ends, servants becoming masters. Money may be an angel of mercy and ministry to God and man; but, worshipped, it becomes mammon

—a god. Aspiration, degraded, becomes ambition; then men are bound to rise, even by trampling others underfoot. If riches increase, set not your heart upon them; gain is loss if it feeds greed. To mind earthly things is perilous for an heir of heaven, for the transient and fading should not, cannot, satisfy him whose true home is the eternal.

Think of the objects upon which human affections so often fix! Can it be possible that a man can be a miser, and himself not become hard, metallic, and irresponsive as the coin he grasps? Can one tread down honour in the dust for the sake of a post of power, or turn love into lust for the sake of pleasure and feel that he is dishonouring manhood? Think of wasting such divine "substance" in "riotous living"! Let every one of us honestly ask what really holds his affections, what practically sways the delicate needle that is pivoted upon his preference. What is it that takes the place of God? A Christian pastor in Britain discovered that on golf balls alone, apart from all else pertaining to the game, more is spent annually than on foreign missions. What discoveries might an honest search make as to the trifles that take up the bulk of time and strength!

What a phrase is that in Psalm 91: "He hath set his love upon Me!" How descriptive of an ideal character! What a pivot is that, on which the whole being may turn! What a centre that, around which all our affections and activities may revolve! Is it not possible for every disciple to approximate that absorption in God, which makes him a little city of God, into which enters nothing that defileth, neither worketh abomination, or maketh a lie? "Keep thy heart with all diligence, for out of it are the issues of life."

From GODLY SELF-CONTROL by Dr. A. T. Pierson, pp. 7-17.

Lesson Eight
HOW CAN THE HOLY SPIRIT HELP ME TO OVERCOME SIN?

It should be obvious by now that if the Holy Spirit were going to act upon man in such a manner as to make man immune to sin He would have already accomplished this in the life of someone—but such has not been and is not now true. Even our Lord learned His perfect obedience by the things which He suffered. Paul presents a powerful struggle in the battle against Satan. Overcoming sin is not then a passive experience. If the Holy Spirit is to help us at all we must cooperate with His conditions to receive His help. His conditions are many and varied.

We could say:

(1) You can have the help of the Holy Spirit in overcoming sin if you maintain *the proper prayer life.* This is so very true but we could also say—

(2) You can have the help of the Holy Spirit in overcoming sin if you *maintain Godly* self control or

(3) If you *abide in Christ* or

(4) If you *recognize the two-fold life* or

(5) If you *live in the Spirit* or

(6) If you know *some secrets of Christian Living* or

(7) If you know what it means to *"Walk by the Spirit"* or

(8) If you will *give up the self-life for the Christ life* or

(9) If you know what it means to be *called unto holiness* or

(10) If we just had *the Spirit directed discipline.*

Perhaps by now you have recognized the titles of several books in the conditions of help we have listed.

It has been the author's practice over more than twenty years to gather a sizeable library of devotional books. Many of these have spoken to his heart and shaped his life. Since there are so many ways in which the Holy Spirit can help us to overcome sin, it shall be our purpose in this lesson to use seven of what we consider the very best of these books (see the bibliography at the end of the lesson) and recommend and discuss from them seven ways the Holy Spirit can help you and me in overcoming sin.

SEVEN WAYS THE HOLY SPIRIT CAN HELP YOU OVERCOME SIN

I. The Christian Life A Participation—Not An Imitation

One cannot make a study of the New Testament without experiencing something of the nature of a shock, in view of the glaring difference between the Christian life as we are wont to live it, and the ideal of the Master. The disheartening incongruities, and the grievous contradictions are so painfully evident, that even those who have only a superficial knowledge of the Saviour's Word—yea, one dare say, even those who have never looked into the pages of the New Testament—are shocked. What little faith they may have, is shaken.

When one holds up before his mind the picture of the Christian life as set forth by the Apostles, and that which today goes under the name, one staggers. The emaciated body of a dying friend—not to say his corpse—could not stand in more violent contrast with him who in the days of health and vigor walked at our side.

It is not my object to pick to pieces the modern Christian. I have no quarrel with the Church. I am not pretending to play the role of an iconoclast. I have been for ten years a missionary of the Cross, and have no thought of deserting the ranks. My only purpose in calling attention to our failure as Christians, is to point the way to the victorious life in Christ for those who are conscious of their spiritual poverty, and "hunger and thirst after righteousness."

It is for the Christian who finds himself at the brink of despair, because of the gruesome picture he presents, when all the while he longs to faithfully reflect the Master's image, that I feel that I have a message. It is for the one whose thirst for the water of life, far from being quenched, consumes him, and leaves him sick with yearnings, that I fain would unfold the secret of the abundant life—the life of which Jesus spoke when He said that "rivers of living water" would flow from the innermost being of those who believed. It is to the one who is wearied of hollow mockeries, sick of shame, who has become the victim of a secret self-loathing,—one who feels that as a Christian he should be free from the power of sin, and who, in spite of all his struggles is crushed by a sense of failure—that I long to bring the message of the Cross. It is to those who pant for power—that power which is from on High—those who long to have their life and service, ministry, and preaching, charged with the Spirit of the living God—that I feel that I have a word which will not fail to usher in a new day.

But we must briefly summarize the requisites of the Christian life before we enter upon a statement of my thesis. We are to walk as Jesus walked (I John 2:6). We are to love our enemies (Mat. 5:44). We are to forgive as Jesus forgave—even as He who in the shame and anguish of the Cross looked down upon those who blasphemed Him, while they murdered Him, and forgave (Col. 3:13). We are to be aggressively kind towards those who hate us, yea, we are actually to pray for those who despitefully use us (Matt. 5:44). We are to be overcomers—more than conquerors (Rom. 8:37). We are to give thanks in all things believing that all things, even those which blast our fondest hopes, work together for our good (Rom. 8:28; Eph. 5:20).

We are to be careful for nothing, but in everything by prayer and supplication with thanksgiving to let our requests be made known unto God, so that the peace of God which passeth all understanding may guard our hearts and minds (Phil. 4:6). We are to rejoice in the Lord alway (Phil. 4:4). We are to think on whatsoever things are true, whatsoever things are honest, whatsoever things are just, whatsoever things are pure, whatsoever things are lovely, whatsoever things are of good report; if there be any virtue and if there be any praise (Phil. 4:8). We are to be holy, for God is holy (I Pet. 1:16). The Saviour said that if we believed in Him, rivers of waters of life would flow from our innermost being (John 7:38). We are to stand out in bold, unmistakable contrast from the crooked, perverse world, blameless and harmless, the sons of God, without rebuke, shining as lights (Phil. 2:15). We are positively to hate ourselves not to pamper, nor to caress, nor to seek, nor to love ourselves, but literally to hate and to renounce our own selves, and that daily (Matt. 16:24). We are told that we cannot be Christ's disciples if we do not renounce ourselves utterly and absolutely in all things, and at all times (Luke 14:26). Paul tells us that our affections are to be set on things above (Col. 3:1).

Enough. We dare go no further. It would only increase our shame, and our pain. We stand indicted. We are not what Christ would have us to be. If this is the measure of the Christian life, if this is the basis upon which we are to be judged, if this is what God requires of us as Christians, like Isaiah we cry: "Woe is me, for I am undone."

Why does not the Saviour, so tender and so understanding, so loving and so wise, not take requirements more in keeping with human nature? Why does He seem to be so unreasonable? Why does He not demand of us what we might reasonably attain? He bids us soar, yet we have no wings. Talk about the super-man; it is not so much a mere overabundance of *man* that it required. It seems to be rather man-deified, if I may so speak, which the New Testament pronounces as the true type of Christian. Why does the Saviour go so far beyond the merely natural, and put Christian living on the basis of the supernatural? I protest, it is not natural to love our enemies; it is not natural to rejoice always; it is not natural to be thankful for the things that hurt; it is not natural to hate ourselves; it is not natural to walk as Jesus walked. Have we honestly faced this dilemma? Have we had the courage to face the implications of Christ's Word? Is anything gained by subterfuges, by pretending that the gulf between the humanly possible, and the law of Christ (i.e. what we can attain by nature and what God requires in His Word) is after all not so great?

If no satisfactory answer can be given (my contention as stated in the following chapters is that there can) the Christian system merits the aspersions of its enemies. It must face the grave charge of over-emphasis—exaggeration—fanaticism—or whatever we may call this want of adjustment between the law of Christ and human nature.

This is no new dilemma. The great Apostle to the Gentiles, makes no bones about this conviction that human nature, as such, can never attain the ideal of Christ. He does not minimize the overwhelming incongruity. He lets the glaring fact of Christ's law as an utterly unattainable ideal, as something to which human nature, as such, can never adapt itself, stand out in all its naked reality.

Romans seven is witness to that fact. Here we have the Apostle's confession of failure, his cry of despair, his bitter regret, upon finding the Christian ideal unattainable, his groanings over what he found to be a heart-rending dilemma, his honest admission that he actually believes that the requirements of Christ's law, are something to which human nature, as such, struggle as you will, agonize as you will, can never adjust itself. Lest I be misunderstood—lest my readers be shocked by something apparently so unorthodox—I quote Paul's own words: "The good that I would I do not: but the evil which I would not, that I do. . . . I delight in the law of God after the inward man: *but,* I see another law in my members (aye, there's the rub) warring against the law of my mind, and bringing me into captivity to the law of sin which is in my members. Oh wretched man that I am! Who shall deliver me from the body of this death?" (Rom. 7:24). Paul struggles. He agonizes. He weeps. He strives as only this moral giant, one of the greatest of all time, could strive. All to no avail. The law of sin, he confesses, like the onrush of a mighty stream, sweeps everything before it.

We do well to face squarely all the shocking aspects of this dilemma. Paul did. He did not throw up any smoke-screen over either his own incapacity on the one hand, or the unattainable character of Christ's law on the other. He is astonishingly frank over the fact that in himself (that is, in his flesh, Rom. 7:18) he can find no good thing. He candidly acknowledges that he delights in God's law, loves it, but finds it something to which human nature cannot attain. If we will be honest about these things, we will find ourselves led all unconsciously to take certain steps which will most assuredly usher us into a glorious new day. It led Paul to a great discovery. It will lead us.

It was not that Paul, when he wrote Romans seven, was still wilfully disobedient, as in the days prior to the Damascan road crisis. He *did* love Jesus. He *was* a soldier of the Cross. He *was* a consecrated Christian. It was only that he was now seeing himself in a new light—in the blinding light of the Cross of Christ. What before, as a strict disciple of Moses, would have been excusable, now overwhelms him with its magnitude. Innocent little things, attitudes comparatively harmless, insignificant little sins which under the Mosaic law would pass unnoticed if they did not appear to be actual virtues, now break his heart. They are repulsive. They are unbearable. They seem to burn with the fire of hell. They sting like the bite of a scorpion. They stink like a decaying carcass in some slimy pool.

Paul wants to be like Jesus. It is no longer a question of mere ethics. It is no longer a question of right or wrong. Is it Christ-like? That is the burning question. Paul wants to be free. Self-love even in its secret forms, its harmless gestures, nauseates him. He would be like Jesus in all the loveliness of his humility, and of his compassion. He would love God with a pure love and serve Him with that utter singleness of eye which characterized the "only-begotten-of the Father." In a paroxysm of self-loathing, and in the anguish of self-despair, the Apostle cries out for deliverance (Rom. 7:24).

Is there a way out? Yes, there is. Paul found it—we can all find it.

Now my thesis is this: we have been proceeding upon a false basis. We have conceived the Christian life as an Imitation of Christ. It is not an Imitation of Christ. It is a Participation of Christ. "For we are made partakers of Christ" (Heb. 3:14). There are good things in Thomas a Kempis' *Imitation of Christ,* but the basic idea is false to the principles that underlie the Christian life. To proceed on the basis of Imitation, will plunge us in just the sort of slough of despond Paul found himself in when he wrote Romans seven.

We are not what Christ would have us to be; the Sermon on the Mount does not find expression in our attitudes; sin as a principle is still rampant in our lives; we are not free from envy, pride, self-love, and lust of pleasure; the mountain of secret selfishness still crushes us and in spite of all our efforts remains immovable; there is little joy, so little freedom of spirit, none of that rapture which so characterized the primitive Christians; we agonize, and bleed, and struggle—but failure dogs our footsteps. What is the matter? *We are proceeding upon a false basis.* We are attempting to do what the Saviour Himself never expected us to do. The Christian life is not an Imitation.

The great dilemma of which we have been speaking resolves itself into most simple terms when we grasp this distinction between Imitation and Participation.

For, what is impossible to me as an imitator of Christ, becomes perfectly natural as a participant of Christ. It is only when Christ nullifies the force of my inherent "self-life," and communicates to me a Divine life, that Christian living in its true sense, is at all possible for me. I must be born again. "The flesh profiteth nothing." Without Jesus I can do nothing. I must live in Him and, renouncing my own life, find in Him a "new life."

Now to this "new life," the Christian requirements, so incomprehensible and unattainable while we move in the realm of the "flesh-life," are all simple. They are nothing more nor less than statements regarding its modus operandi. The Sermon on the Mount so far from cramping in any way this new life, is simply a statement of the way it operates.

The trouble is, we have not listened to Jesus. He tells us that we must abide in Him as a branch in the Vine. Matthew 5, 6, 7, without John 15, would be like so many freight cars without an engine, or like a whale without water, or a bird without air.

In that upper-room interview, the Master, knowing that it was His last opportunity to impress fundamentals upon His disciples, places the supreme emphasis upon this mystical union, this spiritual oneness with Himself of all believers—this sublime fact of participation. *"Abide in Me and I in you."* Our failures only confirm the Saviour's Word, for He said: *"Without Me ye can do nothing."*

No, we are not called upon to imitate Christ. The truth of the matter is, there would be little virtue after all in that sort of thing. Paul said so, in effect, in the oft-quoted I Corthinians thirteen—the love chapter. It could only be a wooden, artificial thing. Even here Jesus would say: "The flesh profiteth nothing." Some years ago in the country where I was doing missionary work, this sort of thing was carried to its nth degree, when a zealous devotee had himself crucified, literally nailed to a cross where his parents found him dead, when they came to his rescue. The Church rightly does not acclaim that sort of thing, and yet theoretically she proceeds, in the case of vast multitudes of her children, upon this false basis of Imitation.

The Christian is not called upon to strain over a role as an actor would agonize over lines poorly learned. The Christian life in the thought of God is infinitely more blessed and compelling. "We are made partakers of Christ" (Heb. 3:14). Exceeding great and precious promises are given us, "that by these we might be partakers of the Divine Nature" (II Pet. 1:4). The Believer is grafted into the Trunk of the Eternal Godhead. "I am the Vine, Ye are the Branches."

"The riches of the glory of this mystery—Christ in you the hope of glory" (Col. 1:27).

From BONE OF HIS BONE by F. J. Huegel, pp. 13-21.

II. The Secret Of Christ's Indwelling

It is meet that the largest church in the greatest Gentile city in the world should be dedicated to the Apostle Paul, for Gentiles are under a great obligation to him as the Apostle of the Gentiles. It is to him that we owe, under the Spirit of God, the unveiling of two great mysteries, which specially touch us as Gentiles.

The *first* of these, glorious as it is, we cannot now stay to discuss, though it wrought a revolution when first preached and maintained by the Apostle in the face of the most strenuous opposition. Till then, Gentiles were expected to become Jews before they were Christians, and to pass through the synagogue to the church. But he showed that this was not needful, and that Gentiles stood on the same level as Jews with respect to the privileges of the gospel—fellow-heirs, and fellow-members of the body, and fellow-partakers of the promise in Christ Jesus through the gospel (Eph. 3:6).

The *second,* however, well deserves our further thought, for if only it could be realized by the children of God, they would begin to live after so Divine a fashion as to still the enemy and avenger, and to repeat in some small measure the life of Jesus on the earth.

This mystery is *that the Lord is willing to dwell within the Gentile heart.* That He should dwell in the heart of a child of

Abraham was deemed a marvellous act of condescension; but that he should find a home in the heart of a Gentile was incredible. This mistake was, however, dissipated before the radiant revelation of truth made to him who, in his own judgment, was not meet to be called an Apostle, because he had persecuted the Church of God. God was pleased to make known through him "the riches of the glory of this mystery among the Gentiles; which is Christ In You, the hope of glory" (Col. 1:27).

"Master, where dwellest Thou?" they asked of old. And in reply, Jesus led them from the crowded Jordan bank to the slight tabernacle of woven osiers where He temporarily lodged. But if we address the same question to Him now, He will point, not to the high and lofty dome of heaven, not to the splendid structure of stone or marble, but to the happy spirit that loves, trusts, and obeys Him. "Behold," saith He, "I stand at the door and knock. If any man hear My voice, and open the door, I will come in to him." "We will come," He said, including His Father with Himself. "and make our abode with him." He promised to be within each believer as a tenant in a house; as sap in the branch: as life-blood and life-energy in each member, however feeble, of the body.

1. *The Mystery.*—Christ is in the believer. He indwells the heart by faith, as the sun indwells the lowliest flowers that unfurl their petals and bare their hearts to his beams. Not because we are good. Not because we are trying to be whole-hearted in our consecration. Not because we keep Him by the tenacity of our love. But because we believe, and, in believing, have thrown open all the doors and windows of our nature. And He has come in.

He probably came in so quietly that we failed to detect His entrance. There was no footfall along the passage; the chime of the golden bells at the foot of His priestly robe did not betray Him; He stole in on the wing of the morning; or like the noiselessness with which nature arises from her winter's sleep and arrays herself in the robes which her Creator has prepared for her. But this is the way of Christ. He does not strive, nor cry, nor lift up or cause His voice to be heard. His tread is so light that it does not break bruised reeds; His breath so soft that it can re-illumine dying sparks. Do not be surprised, therefore, if you cannot tell the day or the hour when the Son of Man came to dwell within you. Only know that He has come. "Know ye not as to your own selves, that Jesus Christ is in you? unless ye be reprobate" (II Cor. 13:5).

It is very wonderful. Yes, the heavens, even the heavens of heavens, with all their light and glory, alone seem worthy of Him. But even there He is not more at home than He is with the humble and contrite spirit that simply trusts in Him. In His earthly life He said that the Father dwelt in Him so really that the words He spake and the works He did were not His own, but His Father's. And He desires to be in us as His Father was in Him, so that the outgoings of our life may be channels through which He, hidden within, may pour Himself forth upon men.

It is not generally recognised. It is not; though that does not disprove it. We fail to recognise many things in ourselves and in nature around, which are nevertheless true. But there is a reason why many whose natures are certainly the temple of Christ, remain ignorant of the presence of the wonderful Tenant that sojourns within. *He dwells so deep.* Below the life of the body, which is as the curtain of the tent; below the life of the soul, where thought and feeling, judgment and imagination, hope and love, go to and fro, ministering as white-stoled priests in the holy place; below the play of light and shade, resolution and will, memory and hope, the perpetual ebb and flow of the tides of self-consciousness, there, through the Holy Spirit, Christ dwells, as of old the Shechinah dwelt in the Most Holy Place, closely shrouded from the view of man.

It is comparatively seldom that we go into these deeper departments of our being. We are content to live the superficial life of sense. We eat, we drink, we sleep; we give ourselves to enjoy the lust of the flesh, the lust of the eyes, and the pride of life; we fulfill the desires of the flesh and of the mind. Or we abandon ourselves to the pursuit of knowledge and culture, of science and art; we reason, speculate, argue; we make short incursions into the realm of morals, that sense of right and wrong which is part of the make-up of men. But we have too slight an acquaintance with the deeper and more mysterious chamber of the spirit. Now this is why the majority of believers are so insensible of their Divine and wonderful Resident, who makes the regenerated spirit His abode.

It is to be accepted by faith.—We repeat here our constant mistake about the things of God. We try to feel them. If we feel them, we believe them; otherwise we take no account of them. We reverse the Divine order. We say, *feeling,* Faith, FACT. God says, FACT, Faith, *feeling.* With Him feeling is of small account—He only asks us to be willing to accept His own Word, and to cling to it because He has spoken it, in entire disregard of what we may feel.

I am distinctly told that Christ, though He is on the Throne in His ascended glory, is also within me by the Holy Spirit. I confess I do not feel Him there. Often amid the assault of temptation or the fury of the storm that sweeps over the surface of my nature, I cannot detect His form or hear Him say, "It is I." But I dare to believe He is there: not without me, but within: not as a transient sojourner for a night, but as a perpetual inmate: not altered by my changes from earnestness to lethargy, from the summer of love to the winter of despondency, but always and unchangeably the same. And I say again and again, "Jesus, Thou art here. I am not worthy that Thou shouldest abide under my roof; but Thou hast come. Assert Thyself. Put down all rule, and authority, and power. Come out of Thy secret chamber, and possess all that is within me, that it may bless Thy holy name."

Catherine of Siena at one time spent three days in a solitary retreat, praying for a greater fullness and joy of the Divine presence. Instead of this it seemed as though legions of wicked spirits assailed her with blasphemous thought and evil suggestion.

At length, a great light appeared to descend from above. The devils fled, and the Lord Jesus conversed with her. Catherine asked Him, "Lord, where wert Thou when my heart was so tormented?" "I was in thy heart," He answered. "O Lord, Thou art everlasting truth," she replied, "and I humbly bow before Thy word; but how can I believe that Thou wast in my heart when it was filled with such detestable thoughts?" "Did these thoughts give thee pleasure or pain?" He asked. "An exceeding pain and sadness," was her reply. To whom the

Lord said, "Thou wast in woe and sadness because I was in the midst of thy heart. My presence it was which rendered those thoughts insupportable to thee. When the period I had determined for the duration of the combat had elapsed, I sent forth the beams of My light, and the shades of hell were dispelled, because I was in the midst of thy heart. My presence it was which rendered those thoughts insupportable to thee. When the period I had determined for the duration of the combat had elapsed, I sent forth the beams of My light, and the shades of hell were dispelled, because they cannot resist that light."

2. *The Glory of this Mystery.*—When God's secrets break open, they do so in glory. The wealth of the root hidden in the ground is revealed in the hues of orchid, or scent of rose. The hidden beauty of a beam of light is unravelled in the sevenfold colour of the rainbow. The swarming, infinitesimal life of Southern seas breaks into waves of phosphorescence when cleft by the keel of the ship. And whenever the unseen world has revealed itself to mortal eyes, it has been in glory. It was especially so at the Transfiguration, when the Lord's nature broke from the strong restraint within which He confined it, and revealed itself to the eye of man. "His face did shine as the sun, and His garments became white as the light."

So, when we accept the fact of His existence within us deeper than our own, and make it one of the aims of our life to draw on it and develop it, we shall be conscious of a glory transfiguring our life and irradiating ordinary things, such as will make earth, with its commonest engagements, like as the vestibule of heaven.

The wife of Jonathan Edwards had been the subject of great fluctuations in religious experience and frequent depression, till she came to the point of renouncing the world, and yielding herself up to be possessed by these mighty truths. But so soon as this was the case, a marvellous change took place. She began to experience a constant, uninterrupted rest; sweet peace and serenity of soul; a continual rejoicing in all the works of God's hands, whether of nature or of daily providence; a wonderful access to God by prayer, as it were seeing Him and immediately conversing with Him; all tears wiped away; all former troubles and sorrows of life forgotten, excepting grief for past sins, and for the dishonour done to Christ in the world; a daily sensible doing and suffering everything for God, and doing all with a continual uninterrupted cheerfulness, peace, and joy.

Such glory—the certain pledge of the glory to be revealed—is within reach of each reader of these lines, who will dare day by day to reckon that Christ lives within and will be content to die to the energies and prompting of the self-life, that so there may be room for the Christ life to reveal itself. "I have been crucified," said the greatest human teacher of this Divine art: "Christ liveth in me; I live by faith in the Son of God."

3. *The Riches of the Glory of this Mystery.*—When this mystery, or secret, of the Divine life in man is apprehended and made use of, it gives great wealth to life. If all the treasures of wisdom, knowledge, power, and grace reside in Jesus, and He is become the cherished and honoured resident of our nature, it is clear that we also must be greatly enriched. It is like a poor man having a millionaire friend come to live with him.

There are riches of patience.—Life is not easy to any of us. No branch escapes the pruning-knife, no jewel the wheel, no child the rod. People tyrannise over and vex us almost beyond endurance; circumstances strain us till the chords of our hearts threaten to snap; our nervous system is overtaxed by the rush and competition of our times. Indeed we have need of patience!

Never to relax the self-watch; never to indulge in unkind or thoughtless criticism of others; never to utter the hasty word, or permit the sharp retort; never to complain, except to God; never to permit hard and distrustful thoughts to lodge within the soul; to be always more thoughtful of others than of self; to detect the one blue spot in the clouded sky; to be on the alert to find an excuse for those who are forward and awkward; to suffer the aches and pains, the privations and trials of life, sweetly, submissively, trustfully; to drink the bitter cup, with the eye fixed on the Father's face, without a murmur or complaint: this needs patience, which mere stoicism could never give.

And we cannot live such a life till we have learned to avail ourselves of the riches of the indwelling Christ. The beloved Apostle speaks of being a partaker of the patience which is in Jesus (Rev. 1:9). So may we be. That calm, unmurmuring, unreviling patience, which made the lamb of God dumb before his shearers, is ours. Robert Hall was once overheard saying, amid the heat of an argument, "Calm me, O Lamb of God!" But we may go further, and say, "Lord Jesus, let Thy patience arise in me, as a spring of fresh water in a briny sea."

There are riches of grace.—Alone among the great cities of the world, Jerusalem had no river. But the glorious Lord was in the midst of her, and He became a place of broad rivers and streams, supplying from Himself all that rivers gave to cities, at the foot of whose walls the welcome waters lapped (Isa. 33:21).

This is a picture of what we have, who dare to reckon the indwelling of "our glorious Lord," as King, Lawgiver, and Saviour. He makes all grace to abound towards us, so that we have a sufficiency for all emergencies and can abound in every good work. In His strength, ever rising within us, we are able to do as much as those who are dowered with the greatest mental and natural gifts, and we escape the temptations to vainglory and pride by which they are beset.

The grace of purity and self-control, of fervent prayer and undertaking in the Scriptures, of love for men and zeal for God, of lowliness and meekness, of gentleness and goodness— all is in Christ; and if Christ is in us, all is ours also. Oh, that we would dare to believe it, and draw on it, letting down the pitcher of faith into the deep well of Christ's indwelling, opened within us by the Holy Spirit!

It is impossible, in these brief limits, to elaborate further this wonderful thought. But if only we would meet every call, difficulty, and trial, *not* saying as we so often do, "I shall never be able to go through it": but saying, "I cannot; but Christ is in me, and He can," we should find that all trials were intended to reveal and unfold the wealth hidden within us, until Christ was literally formed within us, and His life manifested in our mortal body (II Cor. 4:10).

(1) Be still each day for a short time, sitting before God in meditation, and ask the Holy Spirit to reveal to you the truth of Christ's indwelling. Ask God to be pleased to make known to *you* what is the riches of the glory of this mystery (Col. 1:27).

(2) Reverence your nature as the temple of the indwelling Lord. As the Eastern unbares his feet, and the Western his head, on entering the precincts of a temple, so be very careful of aught that would defile the body or soil the soul. No beasts must herd in the temple courts. Get Christ to drive them out. "Know ye not that ye are a temple of God? The temple of God is holy and such are ye." (I Cor. 3:16).

(3) Hate your own life. "If any man hateth not his own life," said the Lord, "he cannot be My disciple" (Luke 14:26). And the word translated "life" is *soul*, the seat and centre of the self-life with its restless energies and activities, its choices and decisions, its ceaseless strivings at independence and leadership. This is the greatest hindrance to our enjoyment of the indwelling Christ. If we will acquire the habit of saying "No," not only to our bad but to our good self; if we will daily deliver ourselves up to death for Jesus's sake; if we will take up our cross and follow the Master, though it be to His grave, we shall become increasingly conscious of being possessed by a richer, deeper, Diviner life than our own.

(4) Dwell deep. There is a depth of life in each Christian soul which is too seldom brought into use. We live too much on the surface, and know but little of the depth that lieth under.

It is related of a slave, pining for freedom, that he discovered a mine, from which he brought ore enough to purchase his freedom. Then it seemed exhausted, and he was threatened with starvation. But returning to it, he suddenly became aware of the glistening of metal in a fresh direction to that in which he had been working. He again took up pick-axe and spade, and followed the new lode, which led him deep into the earth, but made him rich.

Thus in the depths of the spirit's life, where Jesus lives by the Spirit, there are resources which would enrich existence with a new energy, a fuller life, an intenser enthusiasm; they are nominally ours by possession, they may become practically ours by use and dwelling deep.

From SOME SECRETS OF CHRISTIAN LIVING by F. B. Meyer, pp. 55-71.

III. Understand The Heavenly Warfare

"Your adversary the devil . . . whom withstand stedfast in the faith"—(I Pet. 5:8 ,9).

The epistle to the Ephesians contains the "present truth" to the Church. In it God has given us a revelation of His will concerning the Body of Christ and light upon His purposes concerning her. We are in the dark about His dealings with the Church because we understand so little of dispensational truth. We may cry to God to do a thing, but if it is out of line with His dispensational purpose, He cannot answer our prayers in the way we desire. It is made clear to us in the Scriptures that evil men shall wax worse and worse, and in the last days perilous times shall come; when darkness will increase, and settle down upon the earth, at the very time that Christ is raising His Church into the heavenly places, and preparing her for translation to meet the coming Lord.

The Christian service of today is different from what it was five years ago. There seem to be at present two distinct spheres of service amongst God's people—the service of those who are still on the old plane, who go on, up to the measure of their light, and God uses them; but every single soul that presses on with God, *presses on into conflict* which they never knew before.

What we need at this hour is to understand our own spiritual position; where we are, and how we are to work; and then to triumph in the conflict. A tremendous conflict. With what? With "principalities and powers." How is it going to be won? By those who understand taking their right position with Christ, far above the principalities and powers; and by their holding the position of victory in Christ until the powers of darkness are beaten down, and God's people are delivered.

We have had glimpses of this conflict in the unseen realm in the past, but it has been a hard lesson to learn how to triumph in the spiritual realm; and how to get *actually* through into the position of victory in union with the ascended Lord, when the cloud of the enemy has settled down upon, and gripped the spirit, so as to pull it under the force of circumstances and surroundings.

With the purpose of learning something of the spirit-warfare, we will turn to the sixth chapter in Ephesians, and in so doing we will listen to Paul, who wrote this letter from a prison. When he was in a Roman prison, his spirit was in triumph with Christ, in the place of victory, and Paul in Rome, and in prison, is ministering to the Church today. Looking at him from the outside, one might be tempted to say—"Ah, poor Paul, his work is ended." "No, no," he would answer, "there is no defeat in the heavenly places." This is the man who wrote of the highest things that concern the spiritual life of the Church; and this revelation we have in this wonderful epistle of the Ephesians.

It begins with the revelation of Christ seated at God's right hand; and closes with the message of the Christian's conflict in the sixth chapter. Let us look at it, sentence by sentence.

In the tenth verse it says, "Finally," in the margin it is "From henceforth." Shall we read it — from here and now — "From henceforth be strong." Be strong in what? In a spiritual position, "IN THE LORD." You are in Him. Where He is, you are. You are joined to Him in spirit. Do you know it? Well, *live* there. "Be strong *in the Lord.*" Not in your own opinions, not in your own strength, but "Be strong" in a person—and that person the Lord. Have only Christ as your centre, and as your life, and as your strength, and as your power. It is the Lord, the Lord—"The Lord strong and mighty, the Lord mighty in battle." Not in yourselves, not in your circumstances, not in your place, not in your plans, be strong in nothing else but *"in the Lord."*

We need to pause here and go over the steps of the believer's path into the position of victory: To be strong in the Lord for the spirit-warfare of Ephesians six, we must first be "in the Lord" in His *death*. "Know ye not, that as many of you as were baptised into Jesus Christ, were baptised into His death?" You must be planted in His death, before you can be strong in His life. He does not say that He is going to make your life strong. He does not say that He is going to make *you* anything. You are to be planted, be rooted, be deep down in His death, so that nothing can tear you out; so that not all the forces of hell can draw you out of your deep-rooted place in His death—"baptised"—"planted *into His* death"; so that you may be so united in spirit to Him as to "Be strong" in His life. "Reckon yourselves dead indeed unto sin, but alive unto God through Jesus Christ." Then "Be strong in His life, as the ascended One." That is the position for

176

your spirit—not for your body, not for your soul. 'He that is joined unto the Lord, is one spirit." Not a mixture of soul and spirit, but the "soul" poured out unto death, as we are planted into His death so that the spirit is liberated and joined to Him who is the Conqueror and Overcomer seated above principalities and powers in the heavenlies.

"And in the *strength of His might:*" "Be strong in the Lord" means to be strong in the strength of His might. According to the first chapter of Ephesians, the "strength of His might" is the very strength that lifted Christ from the dead, and set Him at God's right hand. That very strength of His might can enter into your spirit, and lift it to the place of victory. Your spirit will never *get* there but as it is actually joined to the One who is there. "In the strength of His might:" that very same strength that lifted the dead Christ from His tomb, and took Him right through the "powers of the air," for He passed through them into the heavens, and sat down. Be strong in that position of the spirit, and in that Spirit-strength which comes from union with Him Who overcame and sat down in the place of victory and power.

Ah, we are so anxious about our bodies. We want our bodies strong, but if your spirit is strong, your body must become strengthened. Your body is not to carry your spirit, but your spirit should control your body. For this the spirit must be made strong by the strength of His might, and this is given by spirit-food. The Word of God is spirit-food. The words He has spoken to us, they are "spirit and life." When your spirit is strong, it assimilates the Spirit-food in the Bible, and you feed your spirit. You need a strong spirit more than a strong body, and even a "strong" mind. Your mind will be stronger, if you have a strong spirit to quicken it, for in that spirit dwells the Holy Spirit. It is the shrine of God. It is the place where God dwells, and the strength of the might of God is to get into your spirit until your spirit is "strong in the Lord, and in the strength of His might."

Have you asked God to make your *spirit* strong (Luke 1:80), and do you use the means provided for making it strong? How? By not only feeding it, but exercising it. A strong spirit comes by exercise. This is why God permits the conflict. Your *spirit grows strong in conflict,* and that is why God permits the warfare. Notice the way in which the spirit gets strong in the Lord: It is given

177

in the eleventh verse of this chapter—"Put on the whole armour of God *that ye may be able to stand* against the wiles of the devil." Does it say "against the wiles of the world?" No. Of the people? No; but "of the devil." Here we see a spirit-position given to stand upon against an unseen spirit-foe exercising "wiles" for some specific purpose. They are to draw you down from your position. If I were able to see into your heart—and you into mine—we probably would find some of God's children have been drawn down. You once knew the song of victory; how to shout the shout of victory, and see the Lord disperse the foe; but the "wiles" have worked around you, and the shout has gone. They have brought to you dark clouds, exaggerated to you all kinds of things, placed pictures in your mind. Wherefore put on the whole armour of God, to stand in your spirit-position "in the Lord" against the wiles of the devil?

Read what comes next: *"For* our wrestling is not with flesh and blood." This conflict is not in the realm of earth, and you are not to walk in that realm. The wrestling is with the enemy back of the "flesh and blood" (Eph. 2:2). Believe me, children of God, if you would learn to attack the foe behind flesh and blood, claiming the victory, in the Name of the Lord Jesus, nothing would stand before you, nor before the shout of victory in Christ's Name.

"We wrestle against." It is a wrestle. It means standing *in spirit* against something that is coming against you *in spirit*. When you really know spiritual union with Christ, you will be distinctly conscious of the approach of this unseen foe coming against you. With the Holy Spirit dwelling in your spirit, there will come in your spirit instantly a sharp resistance springing spontaneously "against" the unseen foe, and your vision will get more acute to detect this. For instance, in practical life, you may meet with someone who will tell you a black story. Instead of taking the black story, you will see the black enemy behind it; and, you will say, "No, I won't take that." That is one way in which you "stand against" the principalities and powers, using "flesh and blood." Our wrestling is against these—against the powers, against the world-rulers. The world-rulers, who are they? But "God rules." Paul says *"against world-rulers."* God is Sovereign *on the throne,* but in this dispensation the god of this age is ruling the darkness;

178

and the darkness in yonder valley where you work is the darkness of the world-rulers. You see it, you feel it. Have you understood how to wrestle with these world-rulers, and triumph, so that you hold the victory, and stand in spirit strong in the Lord and the strength of His might against the foe?

"And against spiritual hosts of wickedness," or, as it really is —"wickednesses that are spirits." There is the drink-wickedness: that is the spirit of drink. The tattling-wickedness: that is the spirit of tattling. Ah, you haven't understood the "Wickednesses that are spirits," when these foes were attacking you, and pushing you to do things that you did not want to do in your heart. All this is because you did not understand the actual cause of the trouble, and did not know how to stand in the Lord, and in the strength of His might, and hold the victory. Here is the spirit-conflict: *"against the principalities and powers, the world-rulers, wickednesses that are spirits."* Then what use is it to argue with men? Deal with the wickedness that is a spirit.

"Wherefore, *take up* the whole armour:" Here we see the action of the will. The Lord does not "will" instead of you. He will do everything for you, but you have to exercise your right of choice. He will give you the power, but you must choose. "That ye may be able to stand." Here is an onslaught of the enemy. There is a "standing against," and in addition to that there is an onslaught which the apostle describes as an "evil day." "That ye may be able to stand in the "evil day." There is an evil day, and there are days that are evil. You rise in the morning sometimes, and you say "this is an evil day;" and so you find it. What will you do? Take the armour, and say, "Lord, I understand that there is an onslaught today, he is working out a plan, there are the indications of it. Now, Lord, I *take* by faith the whole armour, that I may be able to stand in this evil day."

Now, notice in regard to the armour that in verse 14 there are mentioned three distinct sections of the Christian's armour, under the names of "truth," "righteousness," "steadfastness." The very first preparation for this battle is having your mind filled with truth. Paul says *"gird up your loins with truth,"* while Peter explains that it is the loins of the *mind* that are to be so girded— *"Gird up the loins of the mind."* You must fill your mind with truth. You must be willing to have nothing but the truth. No theory or theories. They will all get broken in this warfare. It is the mind you must gird first. If your mind is filled with novels, you will not have any victory, or if your mind is filled with your own thoughts, it is very poor stuff to stand against the enemy. If, however, your mind is filled with *truth,* then, when the enemy attacks you, you have an answer for him in the words of Scripture; and that, too, in a moment, for the sudden attacks of the enemy often give you no time to fetch the Book.

Do you know how to fight with the Word of God, and what to do when the onslaught comes in your private life? Do you know when heavy oppression comes on your spirit, how to break through it all in spirit, by using the truth of God? Do you understand how to wield the victory texts, such as—"The Son of God was manifested that He might destroy the works of the devil;" "that through death He might destroy him that had the power of death, that is, the devil;" "they overcame him by the blood of the Lamb, and by the word of their testimony, and they loved not their lives even unto death"? Begin then with your texts, and use them until your spirit is free, and rejoicing in victory, and you see the conquest of Christ over the foe.

You have been under depression, and thought it physical! You thought you were "very tired;" you said that you had "no message!" You became dumb; when you met needy souls you had nothing to say to them! You thought that you must have grieved the Lord. Someone came to you in trouble, and you could not impart any comfort! Or others came with gossip, "Ah, do you know what so-and-so did?" "As, yes," and so on the talk comes, and you have no power to resist it, and sweep away by a word of light and power the tattling spirits which you see. Then, too, there are the private meetings of the Lord's children when they pass from one to the other the spirit of depression, and the spirit of darkness upon their spirits; which they do not recognise, and refuse because they do not discern the working of the "power of the air" at work around them!

If you are physically tired, that is no reason why your *spirit* should be crushed. You are on the winning side with the victorious Christ, and can afford to wait. Oh, children of God, who know the Living Lord, rise and take your place in spirit "in the Lord," and throw off this cloud that is on you. There is power locked up in God's faithful children enough to shake the land again, if that power could only break through the weight which has come upon it. Were not most of us ignorant when the supernatural forces fell upon the land? Were we not as those who were walking in a strange realm, knowing little what was happening. We did not understand clearly about the principalities and powers, and, in our ignorance, all these dark hosts gathered around, and they slowly stole again upon the land that God had claimed. They stole upon the Church, and upon the living witnesses, and bore upon them the crushing weight of opposition and darkness, criticism, unkindness and coldness.

Much has been learned since then, but oh, souls, have you yet learned to understand how to throw off the cloud of the enemy, and in spirit keep in victory? Then you can live in the darkest place, and live in the light of the Sun of Righteousness. There is a *"sphere above the sphere of darkness,"* and that is your right place. Pember says that the word "the power of the air" means "thick and misty air"; showing that the realm around our planet consists of "thick and misty air" under the control of the prince of the power of the air. Above that is the sunlight, where the ascended Son of God sits waiting for His enemies to be made the footstool of His feet. When you pray "Oh that Thou wouldst rend the heavens and come down," you are asking God to break through the thick and misty air, and by prayer you are making way for Him. He wants a link below . . .

When your spirit gets down into a mist you may know you have been drawn into the lower realm of the enemy. When your spirit is in unbroken communion with Christ, you will know what he wants you to do. The Holy Spirit dwells on your spirit: if you live in the deep stillness with Him, you will come to detect the slightest movings of that Spirit. When there has been no move in your spirit, and you have acted, then things have gone wrong. What blundering babes we have been. How merciful it has been of God to use us. No wonder the powers of darkness have taken advantage of our ignorance; but God has given us light, that we may become intelligent soldiers for a triumphant warfare.

Just briefly let us look at the only aggressive portion of this passage. The 18th verse is the aggressive verse—the climax of the whole, the aggressive weapon of the warrior. *"With all prayer and supplication, praying at all seasons in the Spirit."* It does not say, "on your knees." It does not say "aloud." It does not say "alone"; but it does say *"in the Spirit." "All seasons";* that is to say, ceaseless prayer in your spirit. If you are ceaselessly praying "in the spirit" you keep the enemy at bay. If you are prayerless, you let him in. In this conflict you must always be abiding in victory by prayer. There should always be coming from you a stream of prayer, proceeding from your spirit wherein the Holy Spirit dwells. This is because you are always on the aggressive. Let the aggressive prayer stream stop, and you will find the enemy press upon you.

Think of what this would mean, if you walked everywhere with ceaseless and aggressive prayer. And for whom should you pray? "FOR ALL SAINTS."

Then the Apostle adds, "Praying at all seasons, with all perserverance for all saints, *and for me, that utterance may be given unto me, that I may open my mouth boldly and speak as I ought to speak."* Oh, Paul, I thought you had had a baptism of the Holy Spirit, you cannot require prayer for the opening of your mouth boldly! Ah, friends, Paul understood the conflict. No man shall preach the gospel if the devil can stop him, yet you have left that man in the pulpit without your prayers. You have let the enemy deceive him, and lead him to preach a gospel that is not a gospel". You have blamed the *man,* and you have not understood that the power which has blinded his eyes and drawn him aside was "in the air". He did not know the power of God enough to enable him to resist the forces in the air, and the devil attacked his mind, and put into it all kinds of things . . .

There are men who are wounding the Lord Jesus today, who would cut their hands off rather than do it knowingly. There are men who love the Lord Jesus Christ, who are saying things that are not a gospel from Him, and they do not know it. "And for me, that utterance may be given until me." Oh, children of God, if you see a man preaching the real gospel today, you see a man that the devil will attack to the utmost. He will bring to him every trick possible to switch him off the truth. Pray for God's messengers; pray for the men who stand in the pulpit: pray that they may live in the light of Calvary. Take to prayer, children of God, but take to the prayer of victory, take to the prayer of mastery, take to the prayer that receives what it asks, take to the prayer that can bind the devil, that can deliver souls. May God take us into it, and from henceforth let us "be strong in the Lord, and in the strength of His might," to stand unshaken to this evil day, against the forces of darkness contesting every step of the Church's advance to the place of victory in her ascended Lord.

From life in the spirit by Jessie Penn-Lewis, pp. 4-19.

IV. What It Means To Be Like Christ

The essential thing for holiness of life is to have a standard, and then to live without deviation by that standard. The Lord Jesus Christ has set that standard for us.

"I am the vine, ye are the branches; he that abideth in me, and I in him, the same bringeth forth much fruit; for without me ye can do nothing." (John 15:5).

There is a threefold thing that He shows us here; oneness in Christ, likeness to Christ, the fullness of Christ. We thought together yesterday of oneness in Christ through our positional sanctification.

The sinner is living in that black, infernal trinity; Satan, the world, and the flesh. The Christian has passed by way of the Cross through faith in the atoning blood of the Saviour into a totally new position, a totally new sphere, a totally new trinity. He is in Christ, in the church, and in the Spirit, and thence he is called by God a saint. . . .

We said yesterday the most important question that can ever be put to a human being is this: Where are you? You are either in that black, infernal trinity over which Satan presides, or you are in that glory-lighted trinity over which Christ rules. . . .

Where we are determines what we are. So that is the question with which welcome this afternoon: What are you now that you are in Christ?

Likeness to Christ through Progressive Sanctification:

This thought takes us again to John fifteen, with which we are all so familiar. Oneness in Christ demands likeness to Christ; the branch that is in the vine must bear fruit. The branch that bears no fruit is worthless and is taken away. "Every branch in me that beareth not fruit he taketh away" (John 15:2). What a solemn thought that is for every one of us who is a branch.

The second thought is that no branch can bear fruit by itself. There is absolutely nothing in the branch itself that is productive of fruit, nothing that the branch is, nothing that the branch can do, can make it produce fruit; only the sap of the vine produces the fruit. So the branch has nothing to do but to abide in the vine. "Abide in me, and I in you. As the *branch cannot bear fruit of itself,* except it abide in the vine; no more can ye, except ye abide in me" (John 15:4).

Third, fruit-bearing is progressive. These verses speak of the branch that bears "not fruit," the branch that bears "fruit," the branch that bears "more fruit," and the branch that bears "much fruit." "Every branch in me that beareth *not fruit* he taketh away: and every branch that beareth *fruit,* he purgeth it, that it may bring forth *more fruit*" (John 15:2). "Herein is my Father glorified, that ye bear *much fruit;* so shall ye be my disciples" (John 15:8).

There is nothing static in spiritual experience; every real Christian is a growing Christian. The purpose of fruit-bearing is to glorify Christ. The branch does not bear fruit to glorify itself, it bears fruit to glorify the vine. But only the "much fruit" glorifies the Father. Anything short of that, although it may bring Him joy and please Him, fails to glorify the Father fully.

Now what is fruit? It is Christ in His outward manifestation. "I in you. I in him" (John 15:4). Those words are so simple, you and I could read them over many times yet never sound the depths of their meaning. We could perhaps turn to this chapter and say, "I do not need to read those words, for I know them." So simple, yet the whole of Christian living is in these three words, "I in you." But if you were to underline one of these words, which would it be, the "you" or the "I"? The trouble is, we mark the "you," and the "you" is nothing and the "I" is everything. Only when that "you" becomes a zero, literally a zero, and the "I," even Christ Himself, fills the zero until only the "I" is seen, can we call ourselves real Christians according to the standard set in John fifteen, "I in you"— you nothing but a house of which the Lord Jesus Christ has taken possession, control and use.

Christ Himself is our Sanctification.

"But of him are ye in *Christ Jesus,* who of God *is made unto us* . . . sanctification" (I Cor. 1:30). Christ Himself is our life. "When *Christ, who is our life,* shall appear, then shall ye also appear with him in glory" (Col. 3:4). The Christian life is not merely a converted life, it is not merely a consecrated life, it is not a Christian life at all unless it is a Christ-life.

It could not be more plainly illustrated than by my little wrist watch. You see it is a very tiny thing, and a very simple watch. It is not studded with jewels; that is not necessary for a watch. There is only one thing that a watch is really for; a watch is not an ornament, a watch is to keep time. That little watch would not be a bit of use to me if it did not keep time, for I have to catch trains and boats and attend meetings. The one thing I require in a watch is that it keeps time, and what makes it keep time? Its size? What it is made of, gold or silver? Not at all. It is the works that are inside.

What is a Christian for? Is he an ornament? A Christian has only one value in this world—to reveal Jesus Christ, to manifest Jesus Christ in this dark, sinful world where men do not know Him and do not read the Bible to find Him there. A Christian is an absolutely worthless Christian unless he is revealing Jesus Christ. What enables him to reveal Christ? Anything in himself? Nothing but the One that lives within him, the Lord Jesus Christ —"I in you." It is all that He asks of you and me, to let Him do the living and revealing.

He not only taught likeness through oneness, He prayed for it. Do you recall the last three words of His High-Priestly prayer? "I in them." The last words He wanted that little group, composed mostly of unlettered fishermen, to hear, so they would ring on in their ears and in their hearts and be unforgettable, were, "I in them." And, when He offered that petition, I believe He breathed out the deepest desire of His heart for every Christian all down through the ages. "I in them."

Has that prayer been answered in your life and mine, so that as we move in and out among people we are not seen, but only that living, glorious Christ is seen in us?

Now, we say that is too high a standard. Yes, it is a high

standard, and do you know what we are constantly doing? We are appealing to Christ to look on our circumstances, our environment, to look at our weakness and our infirmity, and to bring His standard down to the level of our experience, and, friends, He will never do it. He has brought us to this hour for the one purpose of bringing our experience up to the level of His standard. Are we going to let Him do it?

The other day I was talking with a man who said to me, "I am not a religious man, I am a pagan." Then he went on to speak of some divinity students he knew who went out to preach in the morning, and then came back and played poker and drank whiskey in the afternoon, and he said, "It does not seem quite right to me; a Christian ought to be Christlike."

That man said of himself that he was a pagan, but he had a standard for the Christian that those Christians did not have for themselves. The world looks at you and me, my friends, and if we profess to be a Christian, it says, "She ought to be Christlike," and she *ought* to be, or else make no profession of being a Christian, for the honor of His name.

Fruit is Christ in us manifested in His glory. But there are so many Christians one can only describe as drab, and I do not like drab. Do you? You do not like a drab Christian, either. We all like to see a glory-Christian. Are you one?

Fruit is Christ in us manifested in the glory of holiness. Now let us bring these two great truths together; Oneness in Christ— "Ye in me," and likeness to Christ—"I in you." The two are indivisible and inseparable. Oneness in Christ demands likeness to Christ. Fruit is Christlikeness, and much fruit is the fullest measure of Christlikeness; and Christlikeness is Christ in you, and Christ in you is manifested glory. Are you in Christ? Then *what* are you? Are you *like* Christ? Are you bearing fruit? Can others see Christ in you? To what measure are you bearing fruit? Only fruit, or more fruit, or much fruit? Would the members of your family know you are a Christian if you did not go to church? Would your friends know that you are a Christian if you did not testify or pray? Would anyone know it if he just looked into your face?

Friends, it ought to be seen. If Christ lives in us, there should be something in the expression of the eye, something in the very lines of the face; we should bear the mark in our faces of the presence of the glorified Christ within. Would one know it from our conversation or from watching our daily walk? When you enter a room, do you cast a chill over the atmosphere, or do you flood it with sunshine? A glory-Christian will flood every place he goes with sunshine, the sunshine of the presence of the glorified Christ. Is Christ the very life of your life?

I am sure that we all want to be Christians who are bearing much fruit, so we flood every place we go with the sunshine of His presence. Some of us came to Keswick for the very purpose of finding out how to live such a life. How, then, may we live it? Likeness to Christ through progressive sanctification requires two things of us, first, a right relationship to Christ, our Sanctification, and secondly, a right adjustment to the Holy Spirit, our Sanctifier!

A Right Relationship to Christ!

To be like Christ requires that we come into a full relationship to the Lord Jesus Christ. It is not enough just to accept Him as Saviour. That is taking simply the first step. We must go on to let Christ become the Life of our life, and above all to let Him be Lord of our life. We read in Romans five of three things that sin did. Sin entered, sin abounded, sin reigned. Sin *reigned*. Do you get the full force of the word *"reigned"*? Sin was absolute dictator over your life and mine; sin possessed us, sin controlled us, sin used us.

But now Christ is our Saviour and we are in Him. Is sin still to reign over us? Are we to continue to live in sin? Inconceivable! Who but One has the right to reign, the One who has been made Head over all things to the Church and to the Christian? Christ now has the right to possess us fully, to control us completely and to use us exclusively. In order that He may do so, He must become Lord. But sin, that stubborn old ruler, will contest His claim every step of the way. But did God make provision for the dethronement of that old Master sin? "Knowing this, *that our old man is crucified with him,* that the body of sin might be destroyed, that henceforth we should not serve sin" (Rom. 6:6).

What does that word "destroyed" mean? To be rendered inoperative. In modern terms, to be put out of employment, out of a job as ruler over your life. And for what purpose is this dethronement? "That we might no longer" serve sin. We have a new Master, even the Lord Jesus, and Him only are we to serve now.

A Choice between Sovereigns:

You and I are called to make a choice of sovereigns. As a sinner we had to choose between our sins and our Saviour, now as a Christian we must make the choice between the continued sovereignty of that old master, Sin, and that of our new master, Christ. "*Let not sin therefore reign* in your mortal body, that ye should obey it in the lusts thereof" (Rom. 6:12).

Have you made this choice? Has it been a deliberate, final choice of Christ as the sole Sovereign over your life? If not, will you do it right now?

Christ Yielded to as Lord:

Having chosen Christ as our Master, then He commands us to yield to Him as Lord. "Neither yield ye your members as instruments of unrighteousness until sin: but yield *yourselves unto God,* as those that are alive from the dead, and *your members as* instruments of righteousness unto God" (Rom. vi. 13).

"Yield *yourselves,*" spirit, soul and body. Yield your whole human personality in *toto* to Christ. Have you done it? Or have you parcelled out a little bit and told Him what He could have, and what you intended to reserve for yourself?

"Yield *your members.*" In order that there may be no loophole, He goes on to say we are to yield every member of the body—the eyes, the ears, the feet, the hands, the lips, the tongue. Have you done it? Perhaps someone here is living in defeat because of one unyielded member of the body. An unyielded tongue, what unlimited harm it can do! Here is our Lord's command, have we obeyed it? Have we yielded ourselves entirely to Him? If not, will you do it now?

Then we must yield everything that has any relationship whatsoever to our life, all our habits, all our practices, all our appetites, our pleasures, our companionships, our home, our possessions, our children, our money.

Last year, after a message on yielding, a gentleman came up to me and said,". . . tonight I have yielded my old pipe." Can

188

you not see that old pipe? The Lord had asked him for it, perhaps many a time. He thought he had yielded it, but he took it home and put it up on the shelf. What he ought to have done with the old pipe was to have thrown it, with everything that appertained to it, into the fire. That is yielding; but, when he saw the old pipe, perhaps he was tempted to think, "May I not take down the old pipe just once again for one more puff?"

Have you yielded your old pipe? It may not be one you put in your mouth, but you may have a blood relation to it, that you do puff away at, which the Lord is asking you to yield. Oh! this is the shame of many even Christian women today! How can you distinguish a woman of the church, the body of Christ from a woman of the world, the body of Satan, if she is puffing a cigarette? What is there to mark her off as belonging to the glory-life?

What is your old pipe, my friend? I will tell you what it is. It is that thing the Lord has been asking you for, for weeks and months, maybe for years, and you will not give it up; that little insignificant thing that is not worth more than the puff of a pipe, and you will not give it up for this eternal Son of God, that His glory may be manifested more fully in you. That is what He brought you here for, to get rid of that old pipe. I do not know what it is, but He knows, and you know. It is that which is keeping you in defeat and it is that which is hindering Him from manifesting His glory in your life today. Will you yield that old pipe to the Lord Jesus Christ. Will you yield yourself, your members, and all that you are and have, to the Lord now?

The Right Adjustment to the Holy Spirit:

This work of sanctification can be carried on only through the Holy Spirit, the Sanctifier, that second great gift bestowed at the time of conversion. The moment you were brought into union with Christ, the wonderful Holy Spirit came to indwell you, and He is there for one purpose, to glorify Christ in you. How does He do this?

The Spirit of Truth who Enlightens

As the Spirit of truth He enlightens us that we may know what we possess in Christ and what Christ possesses in us. Ephesians speaks of a double inheritance, the saint's inheritance in Christ and Christ's inheritance in the saint. "That the God of our Lord Jesus Christ, the Father of glory, may give unto you the Spirit of wisdom and revelation in the knowledge of him: *The eyes of your understanding being enlightened; that ye may know* what is the hope of his calling, and what the riches of the glory of his inheritance in the saints, and what is the exceeding greatness of his power to usward who believe" (Eph. 1:17-19). The Spirit of truth gives up a progressive revelation of Christ and of our riches in Him so that once having seen Him we will want Him and Him only.

The Spirit of Power who Enables

As the Spirit of power He enables us that we may possess what we know to be ours in Christ. He is the power that worketh in us to make Christ a living reality within and to fill us unto all the fullness of God. "That he would grant you, according to the riches of his glory, to *be strengthened with might by his Spirit in the inner man,* that Christ may dwell in your hearts by faith; ... that ye might be filled unto all the fullness of God" (Eph. 3: 16,17,19). The Spirit of power works for a progressive realization of Christ within us as our Life and our Lord.

The Spirit of Holiness who Separates

As the Spirit of holiness He separates us from the world. He shows us there can be no mixture between darkness and light, no friendship between the world and the church. The Spirit makes us know that whoever is a friend of the world is in the sight of God an adulteress for that one has broken the marriage vow to Christ, and by so doing has become the enemy of God. *"Be ye not unequally yoked together with unbelievers:* for what fellowship hath righteousness with unrighteousness? and what communion hath light with darkness? Wherefore *come out from among them, and be ye separate,* saith the Lord" (II Cor. 6: 14;17). *"Ye adulteresses* (who break your marriage vow to Christ), know ye not that *the friendship of the world is enmity with God?* Whosoever therefore would be a friend of the world maketh himself an enemy of God" (James 4:4 R.V.). The Spirit of holiness works progressively to separate us from earthly things and from the love of the world and to strip us of everything of which Christ is not the source, the center and the goal.

190

HOW CAN THE HOLY SPIRIT HELP ME TO OVERCOME SIN?

The Spirit of Life who Counteracts

As the Spirit of life He counteracts all the work of the flesh within. While the Christian is no longer in the flesh, the flesh is still in him and remains there through life. The flesh will do everything it can possibly do to regain possession, control and use of the life. But that wonderful Spirit of life is within to counteract all the workings of the flesh, and when we let the Holy Spirit have absolute control, He can keep the flesh from having dominion and power over us. "For the law of *the Spirit of life* in Christ Jesus *hath made me free* from the law of sin and death" (Rom. 8:2). "For the *flesh lusteth against* the Spirit, and the *Spirit against the flesh;* and these are contrary the one to the other; so that ye cannot do the things that ye would" (Gal. 5:17). The Spirit of life works progressively to counteract the flesh by taking control and by crowning Christ Lord of all in life and work.

The Spirit of Glory who Conforms

As the Spirit of glory He conforms us to the image of the Lord Jesus Christ. As He frees us from the earthly, He fashions us into the heavenly. "But we all, with unveiled face beholding as in a mirror the glory of the Lord, are *transformed into the same image from glory to glory,* even as from the Lord the Spirit" (II Cor. 4:18, R.V.). What a picture in promise of our progressive sanctification! Today like Christ, but tomorrow we may be still more like Christ; every day may see some new touch of glory added to the life and some new bit of likeness to Him may be revealed to those with whom we live and work. The Spirit of glory works progressively to conform us to the image of Christ *from* glory to glory so that we may grow up into Him in all things.

And what is the result of the work of the Holy Spirit, our Sanctifier?

Realized Holiness of Life

We become the Christian who bears the much fruit. "But *the fruit of the Spirit* is love, joy, peace, longsuffering, gentleness, goodness, faith, meekness, temperance (self-control)" (Gal. 5:22, 23).

A wonderful cluster of fruit that cannot be broken! Nine

marvelous, heavenly, spiritual graces that reveal to us the perfection of the moral character of Jesus Christ. And they are to be in us as the work of this divine Spirit in beautiful symmetry and in ever-growing evidence of the life of Christ within.

But how often we see a life that has one of these characteristics in a marvelous way but sadly lacks in another and the testimony of the life is marred thereby. At a meeting once in China, a Chinese doctor was translating for me. She was the largest Chinese woman I ever saw and her heart of love was as big as her body. But in the midst of the message which had brought conviction to her own soul, she stopped me and confessed to the nurses, who worked under her supervision, the sin of so often losing her temper. She had love but not self-control.

Sometimes you will see a Christian who truly bears great trial and affliction with long-suffering, but she has a face as long as her long-suffering. There is long-suffering, but no joy.

Then again you will meet someone who is the soul of goodness, but her face is a mass of wrinkles, made by fretting and worry. There is goodness but no peace.

A while ago after speaking at a meeting a woman came up and introduced herself. Within two minutes she made this astounding statement, "I hope you will not think me boastful, but everything I do is a success." Well, I did not want to misjudge her, but it did sound a bit boastful. She continued the conversation about herself and soon had made this same remark again. She was a woman of faith, quite orthodox in fact, but seemed lacking in meekness. The only memory I have of that Christian is that boastful remark. It set me thinking. What do people think of the last remark they heard me make? What memories do I leave behind me? It is a solemn thought. Have we drawn attention to ourselves, or have we fixed the thought of others upon our glorified Lord? Is there anything in you or in me that is worth the slightest thing? Should not our Lord have all the glory in everything?

Are we the much-fruit bearing Christians? Do we manifest His love, joy, peace, long-suffering, gentleness, goodness, faith, meekness and self-control in ever-increasing beauty and symmetry?

From CALLED UNTO HOLINESS by Ruth Paxson, pp. 41-64.

V. Communicate Christ To Your Children

"And I will betroth thee unto Me forever." Hosea 2:19.

That is a tenderly beautiful figure; surely one of the sweetest and most exquisite in God's Word! "I will betroth thee unto Me forever!" The communion of ideal wedlock is used to express the ideal relationship between the soul and its Lord. We are to be married unto the Lord! Look into the heart of it, and see how much the gracious figure reveals.

"I will betroth thee unto Me forever." There is to be a wedding of the soul and its Saviour, of the nation and its King. To bring that wedding about is the aim and purpose of every kind and type of Christian ministry. We are to labour to bring souls into marriage-covenant with their Lord. I wish for the present to limit my outlook entirely to the winning of the children, and shall engage your thought to the pertinent problem as to how they can be wooed into a marriage-contract with the Lord of glory. What is the kind of wooing that will lead to a wedding?

Let me begin here. I do not think we greatly help the cause of the Lover by proclaiming the remoteness of the Lover's name. I have never been able to find out what we gain by teaching children the "far-offness" of the Saviour's dwelling.

> There is a happy land
> Far, far away!

How does that help the wooer?

> For beyond the clouds and beyond the tomb
> It is there, it is there, my child.

I say, how does that help the wooing? I am afraid that the remoteness of the home tends to create a conception of the remoteness of the Lover and, if the Lover is away, the wooing will be very mechanical and cold.

> There's a Friend for little children
> *Above the bright blue sky.*

That is the only line I don't like in that greatly beloved and very beautiful hymn. In my childhood it helped to make my Saviour an absentee, and He was "above the bright blue sky," when I wanted Him on the near and common earth. I think that we shall perhaps best help the cause of the Wooer if we teach that

His home is very near, and that no clouds interpose between us and the place of His abiding.

There is a happy land,
Not far away.

Destroying all sense of remoteness, we must labour to bring the children into the immediate presence of the Lover Himself. How shall we do it? What is there in the child of which we must lay hold? To what shall we make our appeal? Ruskin was never weary of telling us that the two fundamental virtues in childhood are reverence and compassion, the sympathetic perception of another's weakness, and the venerating regard for another's crown. To perceive the sorrows of life, and to maintain a sense of the dignities of life, are two rare and choice endowments; and, when these are exercised upon "the Man of Sorrows," and "the King with many crowns," the issue will be a life of commanding spiritual devotion. But Ruskin's analysis does not altogether, and quite fittingly, serve my purpose here. It is more to my purpose to borrow the familiar line of Wordsworth, for his teaching includes the teaching of Ruskin, and also adds to it—"We live by admiration, hope, and love." In those three attributes a man's personality abides. Gain them, and you win the man! All the three attributes must be regarded in indissoluble union. The quality of each depends upon the presence of all. Strike out one, and you maim and impoverish the rest. There is an imperfect love in which there is no admiration. There is an imperfect admiration in which there is no love. Perfect love admires: perfect admiration loves; and love and admiration are ever associated with the gracious spirit of hopeful aspiration. These three, I say, constitute the very marrow of life—the deep, secret springs of character and conduct. "We *live* by admiration, hope, and love." To win a child's love, and admiration, and hope, is to grip his entire being, and make conquest of all the powers of his soul. If the great Lover can win these, the wooing will be followed by the wedding. How can we so represent Him, that this triumph shall be won?

We have so to reveal Jesus to the children, that He captivates their love. What shall we reveal to them? Instinctively, I think, we feel that we must let them gaze long at His beauteous simplicity. We must reveal Him handling the lilies; we must strike to make it so real, that the children, with their magnificently realistic imaginations, shall feel that they are with Him among the flowers of the field. We must reveal Him watching the graceful flight of the birds of the air, and His peculiarly tender regard for the common sparrow. We must reveal Him pausing to give thought to the hen and her chickens, and His wistful interest in the sheep and the sheepfold. We must reveal Him as the approachable Jesus, with groups of little children clustering about His knees; not bored by them, not too great for their companionship, but lovingly taking them into His arms to bless them; and, if there is some puny weakling among them, giving to that one some special caress and regard. Will these fascinating simplicities, if vividly revealed, be ineffective in awaking the impressionable responsiveness of a little child? Depend upon it, the heart will begin to thrill! But not only His simplicity must we reveal, but His sympathy too! We must whip up our own powers, and seek to clearly depict for the child the great Lover's love for the weak, the defenseless, the unloved, and the abandoned.

But cannot we go further? Must we confine the visions of the children to the simplicities and sympathies of the Lover? Must we just keep to the fireside Jesus, the Jesus of the lilies, the farmyard, and the sheepfold, the good-Samaritan Jesus, binding up the wounds of the bruised and broken? Shall we keep the children in the "green pastures," and by "the still waters," or shall we take them into "the valley of the shadow'? Shall they abide upon the sunny slopes of Galilee, and watch the Lover there, or shall we guide their feet into Gethsemane, and let them gaze on Calvary? Brethren, I will give my own experience; at any rate, it is one man's witness, and represents, I avow, the findings of one who seeks to woo young life into covenant-communion with the Lord. I sometimes take my young people into the garden of Gethsemane and up the hill of Calvary; I do not do it frequently, lest the *via dolorosa* should become a common way, and should be trod with flippant step; but now and again, when I think I dare, I lead them into the shadow of the Passion, and whisper to them hints of the awful mystery! And what do I find? My brethren, I find that there is no wooing like that! It is not only for the reprobate, but also for the little child, that in the passion of the Lord there is unbared the infinite love of the

Lover. There is no need to be sensational. The sensational is never the parent of fruitful love. Gethsemane was very quiet and all we need to do is to walk very softly, taking the children with us, and let them gaze upon the Sufferer as He bows amid the olive-groves on that most eventful night. The spiritual appreciativeness of the child will supply the rest. "I thank Thee, O Father . . . that Thou hast hid these things from the wise and prudent, and hast revealed them unto babes." "Out of the mouths of babes and sucklings hast Thou ordained praise." I say there is no wooing like this! The spiritual marriage contract is most frequently made in Gethsemane and at the Cross. "The love of Christ constraineth me."

"We live by love." By "admiration" too! Our children must not only find in the Lover their Saviour; they must find in Him their Hero too. Say to yourself, "I will so present my Master as a Hero as to woo the adoring homage of my boys." Would you suffer from any lack of matter? Your eyes are closed and sealed if you do not see the heroic glowing upon every page of the sacred story! His splendid chivalry; His tremendous hatred of all meanness and sin; His magnificent "aloneness" in the night; His strenuous refusal of a popular crown, when the sovereignty would mean compromise with the powers of darkness! Let these be unfolded with the same tremendous effort at vivid realization which we make when we seek to unveil the heroisms of a Cromwell, a Howard, or a Gordon, and our boys and girls will go on their knees before the unveiling with reverent admiration and homage. "Thou art worthy, O Christ, to receive all honour and glory."

Loving! Admiring! These fair dispositions will be assuredly associated with the beautiful genius of hope. The glorious Lord will become the children's bread. Their worship will become their hunger. Their loving will become their longing. Their admiration will become their aspiration. Their faith will become their hope. They will be laid hold of in all the fetters and feelings of personality, and the great Wooer will have won.

What more shall we say about ourselves? Let this be said: while we are employed in wooing do not let us be heedless as to the manner of our living. I know that is a great commonplace, but I know also that it is by the preservation of the commonplace that we maintain the wholeness and sanity of our lives. Those who woo for the Master must be careful how they live. The detection of inconsistency is fatal to the reception of our message. "A child is the most rigid exacter of consistency." "I say" may count for little or nothing. "I know" may count for very little more. "I am" is the incarnation which gives defense and confirmation to the Gospel, and reveals the deputy-wooer in something of the reflected beauty of the glorious Lover Himself. The wooers must themselves be won; and our own conquest must be proved by the brightness and purity of our wedding apparel and the radiant buoyancy of our dispositions. I say the wooers must be in wedding attire, and must be "children of light," children of the morning. "I wonder if there is so much laughter in any other home in England as in ours." So wrote Charles Kingsley in one of his incomparable letters to his wife! That sounds fascinating, captivating, there is the ring of the wedding-bells in the quaint and only partially hidden boast. I do not wonder that this child of the morning was such a mighty wooer for his Lord! Let us beware of a forced seriousness. Let us discriminate between sobriety and melancholy. It was a saying of David Brainerd's that "there is nothing that the devil seems to make so great a handle of as a melancholy humour." Let us distinguish between a wedding and a funeral, and in our wooing let it be the wedding-bells which lend their music to our speech. I confess that in the school-teaching of my early days I think the wooers gave too much prominence to the minor key, and the dirge of melancholy resignation too often displaced the wedding-march of a triumphant walk with God.

When shall we begin the wooing? When I had written that sentence I chanced to lift my eyes from the paper, and I saw a tender fruit-sapling just laden with blossoms. At what age may a sapling blossom? At what age may a young life begin to blossom for the King? To revert to my figure—when shall we begin the wooing? Plato said, "The most important part of education is right training in the nursery." And Ruskin said, "When do you suppose the education of a child begins? At six months old it can answer smile with smile, and impatience with impatience." Perhaps we have to begin the wooing even in the speechless years. In the life of the Spirit I believe in early wooings because I believe in early weddings! The wooing and the wedding become increasingly difficult when we pass the age of twelve. As for the wedding itself, the betrothal to the Lord, I would have it a very decisive act. It must be a conscious, intelligent consecration. The vow must not be made in thoughtlessness; not in any bewildering and sensational transports. In the rapture there must be the moderating presence of serious and illumined thought. But mind you, the act of decision must be a wedding and not a funeral. It must be serious and yet glad.

> I give my heart to Thee,
> Saviour Divine.
> For Thou art all to me
> And I am Thine.
> Is there on earth a closer bond than this
> That my Beloved's mine and I am His?

From THE PASSION FOR SOULS by J. H. Jowett, pp. 38-50.

VI. The Mature Christian

"Ye therefore shall be perfect, as your heavenly Father is perfect." Matthew 5:48, R.V.

In Matthew 5 verses 29-30 and verse 48 respectively our Lord refers to two things which are full of vital instruction. In verses 29-30 He is referring to the necessity of a maimed life: "And if thy right eye offend thee, pluck it out, and cast it from thee"; in verse 48 He refers to the life which is not maimed, but perfect. These two statements embrace the whole of our spiritual life from beginning to end.

"Ye therefore shall be perfect, as your heavenly Father is perfect." God is so almightily simple that it is impossible to complicate Him, impossible to put evil into Him or bring evil out of Him; impossible to alter His light and His love, and the nature of the faith born in me by the Holy Spirit will take me back to the Source and enable me to see what God is like, and until I am all light and all love in Him, the things in me which are not of that character will have to pass. In the beginning of Christian experience the life is maimed because we are learning. There is the right eye to be plucked out, the right hand to be cut off, and we are apt to think that is all God means; it is not. What God means is what Jesus said, "Ye shall be perfect, as your heavenly

198

Father is perfect." When we discern that the sword that is brought across our natural life is not for destruction, but for discipline, we get His idea exactly. God never destroys the work of His own hands, He removes what would pervert it, that is all. Maturity is the stage where the whole life has been brought under the control of God.

I. THE UPWARD LOOK

Psalm 121 portrays the upward look—"I will lift up mine eyes unto the mountains: from whence shall my help come? My help cometh from the Lord, which made heaven and earth." The upward look of a mature Christian is not to the mountains, but to the God who made the mountains. It is the maintained set of the highest powers of a man—not star-gazing till he stumbles, but the upward gaze deliberately set towards God. He has got through the "choppy waters" of his elementary spiritual experience and now he is set on God. "I have set the Lord always before me"—but you have to fight for it.

II. THE FORWARD LOOK

"Thine eyes shall see the king in his beauty: they shall behold a far-stretching land" ("a land of far distances") (Isaiah 33:17, R.V. marg.). The forward look is the look that sees everything in God's perspective whereby His wonderful distance is put on the things that are near. Caleb had the perspective of God; the men who went up with him saw only the inhabitants of the land as giants and themselves as grasshoppers. Learn to take the long view and you will breathe the benediction of God among the squalid things that surround you. Some people never get ordinary or commonplace; they transfigure everything they touch because they have got the forward look which brings their confidence in God out into the actual details of life. The faith that does not react in the flesh is very immature. Paul was so identified with Jesus Christ that he had the audacity to say that what men saw in his life in the flesh was the very faith of the Son of God. Galatians 2:20 is the most audacious verse in the Bible! Paul is not referring to his own elementary faith in Jesus Christ as his Saviour, but to the faith of the Son of God, and he says that that identical faith is now in him.

Fortitude in trial comes from having the long view of God. No matter how closely I am imprisoned by poverty, or tribulation,

I see "the land that is very far off," and there is no drudgery on earth that is not turned Divine by the very sight. Abraham did not always have the forward look; that is why he did a scurry down to Egypt when there was a famine in the land of promise. Why shouldn't I starve for the glory of God? Immediately I fix on God's "goods," I lose the long view. If I give up to God because I want the hundredfold more, I never see God.

III. THE BACKWARD LOOK

"And thine ears shall hear a word behind thee saying, This is the way, walk ye in it; when ye turn to the right hand, and when ye turn to the left." Isaiah 30:21.

The surest test of maturity is the power to look back without blinking anything. When we look back we get either hopelessly despairing or hopelessly conceited. The difference between the natural backward look and the spiritual backward look is in what we forget. Forgetting in the natural domain is the outcome of vanity—the only things I intend to remember are those in which I figure as being a very fine person! Forgetting in the spiritual domain is the gift of God. The Spirit of God never allows us to forget what we have been, but He does make us forget what we have attained to, which is quite unnatural. The surest sign that you are growing in mature appreciation of your salvation is that as you look back you never think now of the things you used to bank on before. Think of the difference between your first realization of God's forgiveness, and your realization of what it cost God to forgive you; the hilarity in the one case has been merged into holiness, you have become intensely devoted to God who forgave you.

From CONFORMED TO HIS IMAGE by Oswald Chambers, pp. 84-87.

VII. Perfect Love

"But whoso keepeth His word, in him verily is the love of God perfected." I John 2:5. "If we love one another, God dwelleth in us, and His love is perfected in us." I John 4:12.

I. IN ABANDONED INDWELLING. Romans 5:5.

There is only one Being who loves perfectly, and that is God, yet the New Testament distinctly states that we are to love as God does; so the first step is obvious. If ever we are going to have perfect love in our hearts we must have the very nature of God in us. In Romans 5:5 the Apostle Paul tells us how this is possible; he says, "the love of God is shed abroad in our hearts by the Holy Spirit which is given unto us." He is speaking not of the power to love God, but of the very love of God itself which is "shed abroad"—a superabounding word, it means that the love of God takes possession of every crook and cranny of our nature. The practical question to ask therefore is, Have I received the Holy Spirit? has it ever come to an issue with me? There is nothing on earth like the love of God when once it breaks on the soul, it may break at a midnight or at dawn, but always as a great surprise, and we begin to experience the uniting of our whole being with the nature of God. Everything in that moment becomes easy; no command of Jesus is difficult to obey. It is not our power to love God that enables us to obey, but the presence of the very love of God in our heart which makes it so easy to obey Him that we don't even know we are obeying. As you recall to your mind the touchings of the love of God in your life—they are always few—you will never find it impossible to do anything He asks.

When the love of God has been shed abroad in our hearts we have to exhibit it in the strain of life; when we are saved and sanctified we are apt to think that there is no strain, but Paul speaks of the "tribulation which worketh patience." I mean by strain, not effort, but the possibility of going wrong as well as of going right. There is always a risk, for this reason, that God values our obedience to Him. When God saves and sanctifies a man his personality is raised to its highest pitch of freedom, he is free now to sin if he wants to; before, he is not free, sin is impelling and urging him; when he is delivered from sin he is free not to sin, or free to sin if he chooses. The doctrine of sinless perfection and consequent freedom from temptation runs on the line that because I am sanctified, I cannot now do wrong. If that is so, you cease to be a man. If God put us in such a condition that we could not disobey, our obedience would be of no value to Him. But blessed be His Name, when by His redemption the love of God is shed abroad in our hearts, He gives us something to do to manifest it. Just as human nature is put to the test in the actual circumstances of life, so the love of God in us is put to the test. "Keep yourselves in the love of God," says Jude, that is keep your soul open not only to the fact that God loves you, but that He is *in* you, in you sufficiently to manifest His perfect love in every condition in which you find yourself as you rely upon Him. The curious thing is that what we are apt, too apt, to restrain is the love of God; we have to be careless of the expression and heed only the Source. Let our Lord be allowed to give the Holy Spirit to a man, deliver him from sin, and put His own love within him, and that man will love Him personally, passionately, and devotedly. It is not an earning or a working for, but a gift and a receiving.

II. IN ABANDONED IDENTIFICATION.

"Love suffereth long, and is kind." I Corinthians 13:4-7. "For the love of Christ constraineth us." II Corinthians 5:14.

The Holy Spirit sheds abroad the love of God in our hearts and in I Corinthians 13 we see how that perfect love is to be expressed in actual life. "Love suffereth long, and is kind . . ." Substitute "the Lord" for "love," and it comes home. Jesus is the love of God Incarnate. The only exhibition of the love of God in human flesh is our Lord, and John says "as He is, even so are we in this world." God expects His love to be manifested in our redeemed lives. We make the mistake of imagining that service for others springs from love of others; the fundamental fact is that supreme love for our Lord alone gives us the motive power of service to any extent for others—"ourselves your servants for Jesus' sake." That means I have to identify myself with God's interests in other people, and God is interested in some extraordinary people, viz., in you and in me, and He is just as interested in the person you dislike as He is in you. I don't know what your natural heart was like before God saved you, but I know what mine was like. I was misunderstood and misrepresented; everybody else was wrong and I was right. Then when God came and gave me a spring-cleaning, dealt with my sin, and filled me with the Holy spirit, I begin to find an extraordinary alteration in myself. I still think the great marvel of the experience of salvation is not the alteration others see in you, but the alteration you find in yourself. When you come across certain people and things and remember what you used to be like in connection with them, and realize what you are now by the grace of God, you are filled with astonishment and joy; where there used to be a well of resentment and bitterness, there is now a well of sweetness.

God grant we may not only experience the indwelling of the love of God in our hearts, but go on to a hearty abandon to that love so that God can pour it out through us for His redemptive purposes for the world. He broke the life of His own Son to redeem us, and now He wants to use our lives as a sacrament to nourish others.

From CONFORMED TO HIS IMAGE by Oswald Chambers, pp. 88-91.